SUCCESSFUL
SMALL GAME
HUNTING

D1551937

M.D. JOHNSON
Photos by Julia Johnson

Published by

 **krause publications**
An F&W Publications Company

700 East State Street • Iola, WI 54990-0001
715-445-2214 • 888-457-2873
www.krause.com

Please call for our free catalog. Our toll-free number to place an order or obtain a free catalog is 800-258-0929 or please use our regular business telephone 715-445-2214 .

Library of Congress Catalog Number: 2003108895
ISBN: 0-87349-524-1
Printed in the United States of America

Dedication

For my father, who knew exactly what he was starting underneath that shagbark hickory some 30 years ago. I can't think of anything more fitting than "Thank you, Sir" except, perhaps, "I love you."

To my Mother, who realized how important it was that I sit underneath that tree…and always encouraged me to do so.

And to Julie, through whose eyes I've discovered an outdoors I never knew existed, and a world I never thought I'd find. Love you.

Introduction

I could take you right there today. Right now. And I'm not talking about the woodlot. Or even the acre in which it happened. No, I'm talking about the very tree where it all started. If, that is, the tree and the woods still stand. Howard Klingeman, former owner of the timber, has been gone for more than 25 years now, so it would come as no surprise if the land has fallen victim to development.

It was a hickory; a shagbark hickory. I was 8, and still torn between excitement and fear. I was also on my own, a hunter, for the first time. Or so I thought. Klingeman's was a big woods — a huge woods. It was full of strange sounds, weird shakings and unseen rustlings. Yes, it was a huge place. Or so I thought.

I didn't hear him walk up. Never did; still, it would be several years before I understood his silence. Softly, he tapped me on the shoulder and signaled quickly for me to be quiet.

"Come on," was all he said. Slowly, in a half crouch, he led me though the whip-thin oak switches and the May apple to the base of a hickory. Twenty feet from the foot of the tree, he stopped and without turning, motioned for me to do the same. And as they'd done a thousand times before my eyes followed his outstretched hand. Beyond his fingers, somewhere among the saw-toothed leaves, sat a door. His door. My door. Our door. The entrance to another world. The first step up to a higher level.

"Let me help," he said softly. Little did he know how much he would help. Suddenly, I could see. Just a spot of rust among the green. Then a tail. An ear. I felt more than heard the click of the hammer. A tiny ball danced silver against the sky. I pulled. The gun pushed. The squirrel fell with a thump. It was an end and a beginning.

Even today I can feel his fingers as he painted the fox squirrel's blood on my cheek, the stock of the tiny single-shot already wet-slick with a matching streak of red. I stood, eyes still wide with a thousand questions about what had just happened, and what was happening.

"It's the way," he said, his voice low. I realize now he was afraid his words might burst the moment the way an errant breeze explodes the milky mist of a swollen dande-lion. "You're a hunter now," he said. And he quickly turned away, perhaps so I couldn't see? Today, some 30 years and several shagbark hickories later, I understand why.

What I didn't realize until some 20 years later was that I was never alone that day in Howard Klingeman's woods. He was right there. Watching. Waiting. Hoping. Maybe even praying for me to do well. And for him to teach well. I have no regrets; I hope he has none. And I hope that I've made him proud.

On a Journey

Take a walk with me through the past, present, and future. We'll go back to Howard Klingeman's woods, circa 1972, and to Eunice Peck's swamp in 1979. Share with me the marvel and wonder of the Washington Cascades in 1993, and crouch in a snowy Iowa fence line in 1997. Trudge the Nebraska sandhills during the opening days of November 2001, and be amazed come the spring of 2011.

See what you've been missing through the wide-eyed stare of a captivated 10-year-old, and silently weep at the faltering steps of a graying houndsman. Come with me on a journey that will take us from the logging roads of western Washington to the alder thickets of northern Maine. From the crags and stone thickets of the Texas Hill Country to the virtual infinity that is Alaska's Richardson Highway.

Come, join this rag-tag collection of traditionalists, dandies, and heritage-seekers, all of whom live for little more than the windstorm flush of a covey of bobwhites, the bawling of a pack of beagles, the rattle of a trap-chain in the pre-dawn blackness, or that give-away flash of a rusty-red tail high in the canopy of a century-old oak.

Make the memories. Share the smiles. With these words and images as both your vehicle and guide, enter the world of the squirrel hunter, the trapper, and the uplander. Walk 1,000 miles in my boots, and always wonder just what is over that next rise or around the next bend in the creek. I hope you'll have no regrets.

M.D. Johnson
July 2003

Table of Contents

Foreword

It is an honor for me to write this foreword. The authors are expert hunters and my long-time friends.

Small game hunting is many things: The challenging shooting of a September dove field, the quiet brilliance of an October squirrel woods, the somber light of a November grouse covert, the excited baying of rabbit hounds on a snow-covered December afternoon—and more. Take the time, and a young person along, to enjoy it. The memories will last a lifetime.

The following is a short story, not a typical book foreword. It's a tribute to my father—now gone—who taught me how to hunt small game. I've since taught my two sons to hunt and, hopefully, they will do the same with their children some day.

I don't believe that my father purposely set out to pass on a hunting tradition to me. Hunting was just something he did. But, just the same, hunting has since become a passion of mine like no other. Thanks, Dad

"The Gift…"

In that fleeting nether world between sleep and consciousness, a sound registered that I had not heard for months. Water was running in the rain gutters of our house. Ice was already melting on that mid-winter day when I awoke. It was a January thaw that I knew wouldn't last. On my way to school the sun was rising in a cloudless, blue, windless sky. By late morning I could take it no longer; between high school classes I called my father at work.

"Dad, you looked out the window much today?" I asked. Not giving him a chance to answer, I said, "Let's go this afternoon." He knew exactly what I meant.

"Just a minute," he replied, and I could see him in my mind's eye glancing out the window of his office and then quickly checking his appointment book. "I'll pick you up at noon," he said, and hung up.

My father was the principal of one of the grade schools in our town, so I knew that education was important. But he'd also taught me that hunting was important, too, and if at all possible you needed to go when the timing was right, even if the time wasn't.

I feigned some vague illness to the school nurse and said that my father was coming to pick me up. Precisely at noon the family Pontiac glided up to the front of the school and I got in. Throwing my books in the back seat, Dad and I grinned at each other as the car pulled away, knowing that for at least an afternoon we'd beat the system.

Hurrying home, we gobbled a couple of quick sandwiches, jumped into our hunting clothes, grabbed our shotguns, and were back out the door in 20 minutes flat. We spent that sunny, relatively warm winter afternoon in the middle of our favorite briar patch. The rabbits were there, as we knew they would be, moving about on the melting snow. If temperatures have been below freezing for a few days—or, better yet, a few weeks as they sometimes are here in the Midwest—and suddenly they shoot up to somewhere around 40 degrees, cottontails will pop out of their burrows like popcorn out of a microwave. We didn't keep any beagles to hunt with in those days, but both of us still managed to take a limit of rabbits. It was the first time that I'd accomplished that feat, and I can remember the glow of it lasting for days.

Dad and I cleaned rabbits that evening until well after dark, both of us knowing that my responsibilities of school and his of the office would return soon enough the next morning. But for those few hours that afternoon and evening we were simply hunters—a father and son with no other cares in the world, except the fleeting rewards of a brief January thaw. And something else happened that neither of us expected. We put behind us the friction that so often occurs between adolescent and adult, offspring and parent. We became friends on that day.

That is one of my fondest memories of my late father. And hunting is one of the greatest gifts that he ever gave me. If you have the opportunity to teach a young person to hunt, don't hesitate. You may be sparking an interest in the out-of-doors that will last a lifetime. Mine has.

Oh, and by the way, the school nurse asked me how I was feeling the next day. "Fine, ma'am," I smiled. "Just fine, thanks." But somehow, I knew that she knew. My suspicions were confirmed many years later when I married a nurse. I found out then what I suspected as a kid—you can't fool 'em.

W. H. (Chip) Gross
Fredericktown, Ohio
June 2002

Acknowledgments

Getting started. That's always the hardest part. Oh, I guess I could start back in 1972, the year I killed my very first fox squirrel, and in doing so joined the ranks of hunters. Or maybe I could start in 1979 with my first red fox. Or perhaps even 2001 when, with friends in Nebraska, I filled my game vest with my inaugural prairie chicken.

Now that I think about it, though, when doesn't seem nearly as important nor as memorable as who. It's the people we share our lives with, and the close-knit band of stranger-friends who call themselves hunters with whom we relate. We are fortunate to share with such people things like a sunrise or a sunset, or the explosion of cattail fuzz as a hard-charging black lab pushes through a brittle November marsh.

These are the people who have made me what I am and who I am. Many hunters and trappers have helped me see life from over a shotgun rib and through the 'V' stamped in the pan a Victor leg-hold trap. How do I begin to thank someone who's voluntarily said without words – "I will give of myself so that you may learn and see and do and enjoy?" It's damn near impossible, but I'm going to try.

This project is for everyone who's touched my life via the outdoors. These are your words and your images, not ours. And though it seems, at least to me, an insignificant tribute to the part of your life that you've given to me, I'd like to say – Thank You. And I hope I haven't disappointed any of you.

To **Howard Klingeman**, Eunice Peck, Bob Wolfe, Sam Gaston, Jimmy Carlson – The folks who owned the woodlots, the goldenrod fields, and the beaver swamps where I grew up…both figuratively and literally. It was your Open Door Policy through which I walked year after year, and I will always be grateful for your generosity and hospitality. And to you Mrs. Peck (1899-1979), thanks for the strawberry pie.

Brad Harris – Lohman's game-calling guru, and a gentleman who still realizes the importance of an afternoon spent chasing a pack of beagles or a seat underneath a towering oak, and passes that torch along to future generations of small game hunters.

Chip Gross – A true friend, devout Christian, and genuinely good human being. I've thanked you before Chip, but I can't thank you enough.

Bill Custer – A rabbit hunter's rabbit hunter, a fine storyteller, and – as my folks were prone to say – "the finest neighbor you could ever ask for." I know without question that you're hunting the Good Lord's Back 40, and even Saint Peter himself is casting admiring glances at that L.C. Smith 16-gauge you carry. Thanks, Bill, for the lessons.

Jim Schoby – Every young man should be so fortunate as to have an Old Man like Jim Schoby. Thanks for letting me skin muskrats in your kitchen, Schob. And thanks for everything else.

Gordy Krahn – Former editor of *The Trapper and Predator Caller*, who took a chance with his reputation and the company's wallet when in 1986 he purchased a short feature story titled *Muskrats in the Deep Freeze*, or something silly like that, from an unknown, soon-to-be college graduate and outdoor writer wannabe from northeastern Ohio. Gordy, did you have any idea at the time what you were getting us both into?

Bruce Knodel – Long-time advocate of hunters' and shooters' rights, and a man who in March of 1972 volunteered his time and made it possible that my father and I might attend and successfully complete our Ohio Hunter Education Course. I still carry that card that my wallet today, Bruce. A simple *Thank You* doesn't seem nearly enough.

Craig Bihrle, Paul Carson and The Ruffed Grouse Society, Chad Coppess, Mark and Terry Drury, Phil Bourjaily – For your wonderful photographic contributions to this project, Julie and I are both honored and eternally grateful. I'm sincere when I say we couldn't have done it without you.

Steve Hickoff, Phil Bourjaily, Doc Erickson, Rob Paradise, Mike Moutoux, Tom Walters, and the aforementioned Chip, Gordy, and Brad – For the time you took to write the introductions…to dredge from the recesses the most wonderful – and, for some, the most painful – of memories. And for your willingness to share those memories with Julie and me and the rest of the outdoor community, I send a heartfelt *thank you*.

And to my beautiful and talented wife/partner, Julie, who never asks, "Where are you going?" when I leave the house with a gun in hand and black labs in tow, but rather says "What time will *we* be home?" How did I get so lucky as to find someone like you?

M.D. Johnson

A .22 and a trio of grays. Is there anything more traditional?

1

Treetop teachers - Squirrels

"I know there's one up there, but I can't see him."

I can remember as a very young boy listening to my Grandpa Farmer talk about making squirrels bark and give away their location. His eyes would twinkle as he ran a coin along a bolt, creating a crude bark. I would not experience his true feelings until years later as I began to call to squirrels aggressively myself.

When I made my first few treks into the wood-lots around my home looking for the little tree-climbers, I had no idea how much hunting it really took to be an accomplished squirrel taker. I thought the squirrel to be an inferior quarry – there for the taking. After coming home many times empty-handed, I began to realize that to be successful at this game, I would need to drastically sharpen my skills and learn all I could about these critters.

Stealth was the word from then on. I made good use of camouflage, fine-tuned my old Remington bolt-action .22, zeroing in my 4-power Weaver scope. I learned patience, standing from 20 minutes to well over an hour in one spot searching for the slightest movement or a small piece of tail or ear. I learned that my ears were as important as my eyes. Listening for the slight rustle of leaves,

dew dripping from a limb, or nut hulls falling from a hungry squirrel's mouth.

I learned to move slowly and methodically, placing my heel down and easing onto my toes. Step by cautious step, I moved towards a likely spot or an unknowing squirrel. In short, I became in tune with the woods, and that is what it took to become consistently successful.

Years later, I employed aggressive calling tactics to lure squirrels to my location. Screaming on a distress whistle to simulate a young squirrel being caught by a hawk or and owl sometimes worked. Barking wildly could also make squirrels do what comes naturally to them – bark back. What a tremendous learning process!

It took many years to realize that the animal I once thought inferior truly taught me to be a better hunter. Everything I learned in those early years paid off big time when I became a big game hunter. The little squirrel had taught me more in my own backyard than all the big game hunting trips combined.

Brad Harris
Lohman's game calling guru
and fanatical squirrel hunter

Julie's Savage .22/.410 O/U - an excellent squirrel piece, and none too shabby when it comes to bunnies, either.

It's a shame. Really it is. These days few people hunt squirrels. There was a time, says a friend, here in eastern Iowa when the opening day of squirrel season was as big or bigger than the opening day of deer AND pheasant seasons, combined.

"That's the way it was," says Dave Fountain, a native Midwesterner who grew up hunting squirrels and rabbits around the town of Iowa City. "Every woodlot had a couple trucks parked at the gate come the first of September. Everyone hunted squirrels. I mean, it was huge. Now, there's woods where I know it's been 20 years since someone has purposely gone in and killed a fox squirrel."

Okay, so that last sentence was mine, but I've said it enough to Fountain that now he uses it. And believes it wholeheartedly.

With the exception of hunters living south of the Mason-Dixon Line squirrel hunting has become a lost art. The people in Kentucky and Virginia, Mississippi and Missouri, they all still know and love the tradition that is squirrel hunting. And that's why some of the best and most knowledgeable all-round hunters come from the south. But the question remains, "Why don't folks hunt squirrels anymore?"

Personally, I think it's a glamour thing. A lot of folks don't see any hype involved in squirrels and squirrel hunting. There's no category in the Boone & Crockett books for a 170-class fox squirrel. And there's no conservation agency with a catchy name like Squirrels Unlimited, Delta Squirrels, or the National Wild Squirrel Association.

Today, most folks would much rather say – "I killed a 12-pointer last Saturday!" Few people belly up to the bragging table and state matter-of-factly, "Yes, sir, I dropped a limit of squirrels today."

And then there's the time factor. In this modern, Oh-My-God, I'm-late-again world in which we live, we all have shorter and shorter windows of time in which to participate in those activities that aren't directly related to earning a living. We simply don't have that much spare time to hunt anymore. And so, with what time folks do have, they choose not to hunt something as mundane and unexciting as squirrels, but instead opt to pursue the bigger game –whitetails and wild turkeys, mallards and Rocky Mountain elk. This is all good; that is, until we're left with a generation with no idea what squirrel hunting is, and how the skills learned in the squirrel woods connect with all that is hunting – **regardless** of that which is being hunted.

Whew! Okay, now that I've said all that, we're going to pick ourselves up out of this no-squirrel rut, go back to Stage One, and relearn everything that we should have learned or everything we've forgotten since we first sat underneath that shagbark hickory with G'pa or Pop back oh-so-many years ago. And if you've never hunted squirrels – well, welcome aboard! I hope that you'll soon understand what I'm talking about when I say –

1. The best all-round hunters I know were and still are first and foremost, squirrel hunters, and –
2. The finest teachers I've ever had were squirrels.

Our largest squirrel subspecies, the fox squirrel, a.k.a. the red squirrel.

Gray squirrels, such as the one perched here, are known in some locales as cat squirrels, a name bestowed due to the variety of cat-like sounds they can make.

Julie photographed this pine squirrel, or chickaree, in southwest Washington, where these small critters are numerous…and as irritating as their Eastern cousins.

Meet the players

The word *squirrel* is a rather generic term, sort of like goose or deer or turkey. Just like there are several different kinds of geese, there are several different species and subspecies of squirrels. And while there exists a handful of varieties outside the boundaries of North America, here in the United States, we're dealing with just five.

Fox squirrels – Our largest tree squirrel, and the one that I grew up hunting in northeastern Ohio is the fox squirrel. During my formative hunting years, we had nothing but fox squirrels in the northern half of Ohio. Gray squirrels were creatures of the southern portion of the state. But today we see almost as many gray squirrels as we do fox squirrels around my hometown of Newton Falls. And in some places, the more aggressive gray squirrels now dominate the population. For those who don't know him, the fox squirrel, also known in parts of the country as the red squirrel, will weigh a pound or a pound and a half, and stretch 20 to 24 inches from nose to tail tip. He's a rusty red-brown overall, with a little black, gray, and white thrown in for good measure. Fox squirrels are found from the Plains States to the East Coast, and from the Great Lakes to south Texas.

Gray squirrels – There are actually three different subspecies in the gray squirrel family – the western gray squirrel found along the West Coast and north into central Washington; the eastern gray squirrel, which makes its home roughly from the Missouri River east to the New England States and down into Florida; and the Arizona gray squirrel, a subspecies that calls – surprise! – Arizona and New Mexico home. Other than distribution, the differences are slight. Size-wise, each will measure about 18-20 inches from stem to stern, and will weigh a little less than a pound. All are predominantly gray in color; however, the eastern gray squirrel often does show a bit more rusty-red or brown than do the others, particularly along his sides. Interestingly, the black squirrel is a genetic color variation of the ordinary gray squirrel.

Abert's squirrel – I had the good fortune of seeing the Abert's squirrel while visiting my grandparents in Colorado, and all I can say is – cool! With tassled ears, striking black-and-white markings, and an incredible gray-and-white tail plume, the Abert's is nothing short of beautiful. This particular species can be found not only in Colorado, but parts of New Mexico and Arizona as well.

Red squirrel – I used to say I hated red squirrels. They were always spotting me as I tried to stalk close to either of their larger cousins, attempts that were more often than not foiled by the red's infernal high-pitched barking. Or, after spotting movement high atop a beech tree, I would creep underneath, only to discover that the beast rummaging about the treetops was a red squirrel. Today, I find the little things that the late Jim Schoby called *fairy diddles* rather amusing, though I'm not above potting one or two both for the skillet **and** out of spite. Small and skinny, red squirrels are just that – red, the only other colors being a white belly and a tail that looks a little like a fox squirrel's. About a foot long, reds typically won't weigh much more than 10 to 12 ounces, if that; however, if you've ever had one scold you non-stop from 30 feet above the timber floor, you'll swear that half that weight is lungs. Red squirrels inhabit the northern forests in the Upper Midwest, New England States, Canada, and into parts of Alaska, although good populations can be found along the Divide from Idaho south into New Mexico and Arizona.

Douglas' squirrel – We called them pine squirrels in Washington, perhaps because we were always finding them in pine trees; however, most folks referred to them as chickarees. Regardless, no one paid them much mind, unless they were getting into attics and wall spaces and storing pinecones, because there is no squirrel season in Washington. Still, the noisy little red squirrel clones of the Pacific Northwest and northern California are entertaining to watch.

Squirrels, and the tactical approach

The way I was taught to hunt squirrels back in the early 1970s was identical to the way my father was taught to hunt squirrels in the mid-1950s. Basic approach involves sitting. You walked into the woods – in his case, he walked out the back door, across the cornfield, and into the family timber – you found a place that looked promising, and you sat. And you watched. And you sat. And you watched.

You watched all kinds of things. And you learned. You learned how to recognize and identify different birds; simply by the way they flew. You discovered that groundhogs do climb trees; however, you never found out exactly *why* a groundhog would want to climb a tree. You learned how to be quiet, and how to move without hurrying. You learned the art of listening and how to not only look, but to see. And then you learned definition of the word, patience. But perhaps most of all, you learned the art of pulling a single grain of sand out of the millions that make up a beach. Almost without your knowledge, you became a hunter.

A retired high school biology teacher, my Father – Mick – has been hunting squirrels in our home state of Ohio for the past 52 years. His squirreling career, he says, began with an old Harrington & Richardson .410 single-shot (I shot my first squirrel with that very gun in 1972). Today, he still carries that gun into the field on perhaps half of his outings. The other half sees him toting a lightweight Mossberg 20-gauge pump. Each year, he hunts from the time the Ohio Department of Natural Resources says he can – though he thinks August is a bit early, what with the leaf cover and all – up until the ODNR tells him he has to quit. When it's all said and done, he'll clean his little squirrel guns, package up his tails for the folks at MEPPS, and go into a sort of funk. A squirrel withdrawal would be as near as I can come to describing it. Once a week during this period of involuntary squirrel hunting abstinence, I'll hear the Old Man say – "You know. If I had to give up hunting except for one thing, it'd be squirrels. No question about it." That's always impressed me.

With that, I figured that we all – myself included – could learn a thing or two from this man with the passion for the sport – no, the art – that is squirrel hunting. So without further ado, I give you my father, starring in *Interview With A Squirrel Hunter.*

Me: So, what is it about squirrel hunting? I mean, there's not much in the way of glamour. So it's got to be something else, eh?

Pop: It combines a little bit of all of the other hunting sports. I mean you're getting up early in the morning watching the woods more or less come awake. That's the aesthetic part of the thing. But the techniques you use

"If I had to give up every form of hunting but one," says Mick Johnson, my Pop, pictured here. "I'd still keep squirrel hunting." Now that's dedication.

Cut pin-oak acorns - a sure sign that bushytails are about.

A leaf nest, this one built by a young fox squirrel in an elm on our place. Leaf nests are commonly used during the heat of summer, but where den trees are few, they can be used year-round.

while you're squirrel hunting are pretty much the same regardless of the species you're hunting. First of all, you pick a good location. That's the key.

Me: Maybe it's a simple question, Pop, but what are you looking for when you're looking for squirrels? And with that in mind, are there any differences between, well, scouting on public land versus private land?

Pop: There's different techniques that you can use for both private and public land. I'd say that anyone's who's new to a public area would be smart to check in with the personnel on the area. And most of them are more than happy to point things out. Like Waterloo, for example. Years ago, they used to keep a big area map with pins in it that showed where squirrels were shot. They had color-keyed maps, with different colors for one and different colors for two and so on. You can do that. Or if you want to do a little scouting on your own, well, the basics are always the same with squirrels. You look for dens. You look for mast. You look for signs of squirrels feeding – cut hickory nuts, acorns, whatever, but it's basically the same regardless of the woods. I'll tell you what. You give me the perfect woods, and it's going to have mast crops. In our area (northeast Ohio), you're going to have pin oak, beech, hickory, and to top it all off, if you have some mature, old maples – they make one of the best den trees. I've shot literally hundreds of squirrels off of old maple den trees. Add water, and there's going to be squirrels there.

Me: Okay, fox squirrels versus gray squirrels; any dif-

ference, strategy wise?

Pop: Without a doubt, a fox squirrel is a lot easier to hunt than a gray. And a gray is a lot easier than a black. It's just by nature. A fox squirrel tends to be slower. They're also a lot more curious, and sometimes he'll let his curiosity get ahead of his survival instincts. You run one up a tree. You wait long enough, and he's going to move. He'll come looking for you. Or if you sit quietly, he'll forget you're there and start going about his activities. A gray on the other hand – nine times out of 10, if he sees you, he's going to move. And he'll go through the treetop. I've seen a gray squirrel go through the treetops faster than a rabbit can run. Or he'll come out of the tree, down to the ground, and he's gone, usually with the tree between you and him. The black squirrel seems to share a lot of the same traits as the gray, but yet they'll hide. And I mean trying to wait out a black squirrel is an exercise in patience.

Me: So you're saying black squirrels are tough?

Pop: With the black squirrel, it's probably in-bred. He knows…it's something about his black coat that he knows makes him more visible. You get a gray squirrel plastered against a beech tree, for example, or against an old pin oak and he can blend in pretty well. Poor old fox squirrel, except in the fall when the hardwoods change and everything turns to orange-red, they're very visible. A black on the other hand, with the same instincts as a gray and the same habits – it's something that they know. They love to hide in the crotch of a tree. Very seldom have I ever found

A black squirrel alongside the more common gray. Often found together, blacks are a color phase, not a separate subspecies.

black squirrels, especially the older blacks, come out on a limb. Most of them like to hide in the shadows, like in the crotch of a tree. I think it's a survival trait. I've seen it happen too many times for it to be just a coincidence.

Me: Used to be, Ohio's squirrel season always began the weekend after Labor Day. Now, Ohio opens in mid-August. States like Kansas and Missouri, they open in June. I hear that's so the school kids can take advantage of the season *before* school starts. But it's hot then. Do squirrel do much this time of year?

Pop: Squirrels are like people. They tend to move in the morning when it's cool. I'd say from daybreak to about 10 o'clock is probably the best hunting on a normal warm September day. Now if you get an overcast, cooler day in September, they'll tend to move all day. Best times there are probably first thing in the morning, and then again from 3 p.m. or 4 p.m. until dark. Squirrels can be active all day. Best in the morning and evening, but on a reasonably cool day, they'll spend the middle part of the day – you might say – just dinking around.

Me: What's the most challenging time of the year to squirrel hunt? Late-season cold? Or early season leaf cover?

Pop: Probably the toughest time of the year is when the leaves start changing. Here, the leaf coloration can help hide the fox squirrels. Plus you tend to have a lot more physical motion in the woods. Leaves falling. Sticks falling. And this makes for a little more disturbance in the

September squirrel hunting can be hot, thirsty work. Military web gear is just one way to pack a canteen into the field. And the many pockets come in awful handy, too.

Julie's eldest son, Adrian, with a late-season fox squirrel. Lack of leaf cover can make late-season hunting an 'easy-difficult' proposition.

Clad in blaze orange - and I'm a firm believer in it - good friend Chip Gross searches the canopy for another bushytail.

woods that then makes it a little more difficult to pick out any movement. The squirrels? I think they're probably used to all this movement, but it just makes it a little harder for the hunter. Now on a quiet windless morning, sometimes this seasonal change can help. I mean, you're sitting there and all of a sudden a bunch of leaves start falling that, well, shouldn't really be falling. But on a day when there's even a little bit of wind, you have all that leaf movement – and it adds a little more interest to the hunt.

Me: You hunt from September through February. Do you change tactics as the season progresses?

Pop: Not really. I tend to sit, as long as the bulk of the leaves are on the trees; maybe September through later October. Then as the leaves fall and the woods get more barren, I do a lot more still-hunting. It opens itself up to it, and I kind of enjoy it. You can see longer distances. For instance, I'll get on a deer trail or in a creek bottom, and just kind of work my way in the direction I want to go. Periodically, every two or three minutes, I'll stop. All the undergrowth is gone, and if you move slowly and take your time, squirrels really don't seem to pay much atten-

tion to something that's moving IF it's moving in the right manner. Go slowly. Take your time. Actually do more standing and looking. You'll pick squirrels up from a much greater distance than you would if you were sitting someplace with the leaves on the trees.

Me: How did you learn to *see* squirrels? I mean **r-e-a-l-l-y** pick them out of everything else?

Pop: Squirrels usually, especially in the mornings and evenings — feeding times — are very, very active. They're jumping from limb to limb. They're running around on the branches. After you've hunted squirrels for a number of years, you get used to the rhythm of the woods and the wind. For example, leaves blow in a certain manner. Branches move in a certain manner. What you want to look for is that abnormal movement; on a limb, for example. All of a sudden, a limb will give an unnatural dip. Or the wind will be blowing gently and the leaves will be moving gently, then all of a sudden, one little group starts wiggling all over the place. That can only indicate squirrel. Okay, occasionally a big bird like a crow or a jay, both of which love beechnuts and acorns, will fool you. But

It's 90 degress, with 98 percent humidity. What would you do if you wore a fur coat?

Years ago, I began carrying compact binoculars into the squirrel woods. Today, I wouldn't think of heading afield without them.

nine times out of 10, any abnormal leaf movement will give a squirrel away. Nuts dropping. Green leaves falling. When the young squirrels start building nests. A quiet morning, for instance, and all of a sudden, a bunch of green leaves fall. That means squirrel. You're sitting in the woods, and you catch a glimpse of something moving up, that is movement against a tree moving up. Automatically that should ring a bell 'cause nothing normal in the woods would be moving up.

At this point, our backyard conversation was interrupted by the appearance of a rather large and exceptionally rotund fox squirrel. Walking in the odd, stiff-legged manner that squirrels use when they're not exceptionally hurried, this old veteran made his way first to a small locust at the edge of our property before laboriously pulling himself paw over paw up into the ash that served as our shade. There, he plopped down on a limb, all four legs pointed toward the ground, seemingly oblivious to the men and black lab dogs below. Ah, my father commented, the life of a town squirrel. Urban rodent or no, the unconcerned fox squirrel nonetheless commanded a

portion of my Old Man's attention. A goodly portion. I wouldn't have been surprised if he had asked for the Crosman pellet rifle we keep secreted behind the front door; you know, for garden-eating cottontails and the occasional bad kitty that happens to wander through the yard. You have to watch my Old Man when it comes to squirrels. But I digress.

Me: Describe the toughest squirrel-hunting situation you face.

Pop: A squirrel will spend the majority of his day on the ground. He'll feed in the tree. And obviously, he'll sleep in the tree. But if you get a windy day in September or early October, with the leaves on the trees and the undergrowth still high and leafed out – well, that makes for as tough a hunt as you can get. That pretty much negates any different signs of squirrel activity. Basically, you *have* to see the squirrel. That makes it tough. Usually on a day like that, I'll hang it up about, oh, 10 o'clock, unless I'm in a woods – say – that cows run. In other words, a mature stand with little underbrush. There you can do well, but in a mixed woods with a lot of undergrowth, a lot of

December, and there's snow on the ground in Ohio. Don't think for a minute that a little white and cold keeps my Pop and his .410 out of the squirrel woods.

My 'research' has shown that squirrels pay little or no attention to a blaze orange cap - all the more reason to wear one whenever you're in the field.

leaves, and a lot of wind....ah, that makes for a long day.

Me: You squirrel hunt even after the snow flies. How does the coming of winter affect squirrel behavior?

Pop: As winter comes, I think squirrels keep up their activity. In fact, they may increase their activity because their metabolism increases and they have to eat more. I think they're more active. You get a sunny day with snow on the ground and squirrel activity goes on almost from daylight to dark. You can shoot squirrels basically any time of the day. They have to work harder. They can't go up in a loaded hickory or a loaded oak, and sit there and just munch. They have to literally go from place to place and dig it up.

Me: Tell me about Midwest squirrels and cornfields.

Pop: A good cornfield, especially one where the stalks were knocked down and there's still a bunch of corn on the ground, can be a honey hole; a real prime spot. My favorite place in this kind of situation is right on the inside edge where I can see down the field edge, say, 50 or 60 yards, if that's at all possible. There you can watch for any activity coming in and out of the field. A lot of times, if there's enough of the stalks still standing, it can be hard to see any distance out into the field unless there's a real, real heavy snow. So your best bet is to stay just inside the woods.

Me: Let's switch gears. Or rather, tell me about gear. Like clothing. We've always worn complete camouflage when we'd squirrel hunt. Necessity? Or fashion state-

ment?

Pop: As far as camouflage for squirrel – well, camo would help. On the other hand, I've had squirrels come up to within 2 or 3 feet of me while I'm wearing a full blaze orange coat and hat. I really don't think that squirrels pay that much attention to an object that's not moving. In other words, if you sit still, I really don't think that camo is all that critical.

Me: Blaze orange. Yes, or no?

Pop: If I'm in a woods where I'm pretty sure that there won't be any other hunters, which in the case of squirrel hunting in our area anymore is very, very likely, then I'll tend to wear whatever the mood dictates. On public hunting areas, I'll invariably wear a blaze orange hat at the very least. That's a must. Again, I've never had it (blaze orange) make much difference. As long as you sit still, squirrels don't seem to pay much attention.

Me: Okay, another turn. Guns.

Pop: As far as guns, a lot of guys hunt with .22s. I tend to lean toward the shotgun side of things myself 'cause it makes me feel a little safer in the areas that I typically hunt. Small woodlots tend to have homes within short distances, and I just feel safer with the short-range limitations of a shotgun. Now down on some of your larger public hunting areas like you'd find in the southeastern part of the state (Ohio), .22s would be okay. Also because so many of the squirrels you're going to shoot are on the ground, especially later in the morning or early in the

A pair of pet .22 rifles, a Winchester M9422 topped with a 4-power Tasco (above), and a Ruger 10/22 sporting a 3-9x Simmons Sharpshooter.

afternoon, a shotgun just makes me feel a little bit better from a safety standpoint.

Me: Gauge?

Pop: I have an old .410. It's my first single-shot, and I've killed untold numbers of squirrels with that gun. I like, though, a 20-gauge. I carry a 20-gauge Mossberg today. You know, just because you originally start out on a squirrel hunt doesn't mean, especially later in the season once the traditional small game seasons open, that it's going to stay a squirrel hunt. I mean we've had squirrel hunts that turned out to be a complete bust but ended up great rabbit hunts. For example, Ben and I went out to Bob's one morning. Hunted all morning and shot one squirrel, but ended up shooting five rabbits on the way back to the truck. I can remember several occasions down at Waterloo when I killed a couple squirrels, a couple grouse, and a couple rabbits before I got back to the parking lot.

Me: Shot size?

Pop: I prefer #6 shot. I've had the most luck with it on early squirrel when their fur is still pretty sparse. And then later when they get their winter coats, I've found that #6s still do the job well. It gets through the fur without balling up, and I've just had no problem with it. The copper-plated #6s are the best all-around. Number 5s are acceptable, but you just don't need #4s. Fours tend to…well, you get too much meat damage with #4s. Let's face it. You're going to shoot a lot of squirrels up close.

And as far as anything smaller than #6s such as #7.5s; there you're going to end up with a pretty good pellet count per pound of meat.

Me: Here's one. Squirrel calls.

Pop: Number one, I've hunted squirrels for over 50 years and have never really been in a situation where I thought a squirrel call would have been of any benefit. Most important, though, I would be very, very leery, especially with a camouflage outfit on, of sitting up against a tree and making a squirrel barking sound. And I feel the same way on a public area, and even on private land because while you can have a good idea that there won't be anyone else there, you're not 100 percent sure. And let's face it; to a squirrel hunter who's hunted any length of time, a squirrel bark is unmistakable. It's like a pheasant cackling. You hear a squirrel barking and you know it's a squirrel barking. And I really don't want to draw attention to myself using a squirrel call. The techniques I use have proven themselves over the years, and I just never have found a squirrel call necessary.

At this point, we'll turn to Brad Harris. In addition to being the game-calling guru for Lohman Game Calls, based in Neosho, Missouri Harris is also one of the most traditional hunters that I've had the pleasure of spending time with. Just what do I mean by *traditional*? Well, he dearly loves beagles and rabbits, and, like my father, would probably give it all up if he had to; that is, except for squirrel hunting.

A bellows-type squirrel call, this one courtesy of Lohman Game Calls.

To call, or not to call. That 'tis the question. Mick Johnson says "no need." Harris claims that calling can be very productive. Your decision.

Knowing Brad will not be far from a call of some kind at any given moment, I asked him a handful of questions about that squirrel hunting tactic to which my father lends little credence. Not surprisingly, Harris had good things about this often effective, but sometimes foreign, squirrel-hunting strategy.

Me: What's your take on squirrel hunting, Brad?

Harris: To me, squirrel hunting is the whole package. It sharpens all the senses. That's what I like about squirrel hunting. It really tests your skills. A lot of people think – "Squirrels? Yeah, I got 'em in my backyard. I can just stand out on the deck and shoot one." That's not squirrel hunting. Squirrel hunting is going into the timber, and locating squirrels at different times of the year as they are feeding on different food sources. And it IS a hunt, and it sharpens everything. It sharpens your eyesight. It sharpens your hearing. It sharpens your instincts. It sharpens your stalking abilities. It sharpens your shooting abilities. It sharp-

ens your patience. So that's what I like about squirrel hunting. If there ever was an animal that will train you to be a big game hunter, it's that little bushytail. The best hunters I know, and you won't read any of their names in books or magazine articles, are avid and very good squirrel hunters. And the techniques that they've learned by consistently harvesting limits of squirrels from May through December….these guys, well, their hunting skills are just phenomenal.

Me: You're recognized more for your turkey calling – first – followed by predators, whitetails, waterfowl, and elk, and it's been written that you've practiced recreating these sounds from a young age. But what about squirrels and squirrel calling? Where'd that come from?

Harris: My Grandpa sowed the seed for us calling squirrels. He taught us at a very young age that you can make noise in the squirrel woods and be successful. But hunting with my Dad and two older brothers – those were the guys that I hunted with and where I learned a lot about squirrel hunting and hunting in general. The first time I had ever seen or heard anything about squirrel calling – well, I was just 8 or 9 years old, and was listening to my Grandpa talk about taking a stove bolt and a washer or sometimes just a little cedar strip. And he would "bark" on that thing by smacking that striker against that bolt. And he used that to make squirrels curious—to make squirrels bark—to make squirrels move. Whatever – whatever. So he was the first one that I ever heard talk about calling squirrels. And so I scraped on a lot of bolts when I was a kid, and tried to figure out this calling thing.

Me: So tell me this – why do squirrel calls work? Or better, what do you want them to do?

Harris: Squirrels are vocal animals. They do bark, generally out of excitement or out of curiosity. Maybe they bark to alert other squirrels to danger. So when they bark, other squirrels are certainly going to take notice. Why squirrel calls work really depends upon the situation you're in. Sometimes it's a confidence call. Little soft barks will make squirrels move to take a look. Or I've watched squirrels go into holes and I've backed off and sat down. I've just waited a little while, done a little soft barking, and curiosity kills the cat sometimes. Sometimes during the "rut," or when they're breeding, squirrels can be very aggressive. They're looking for that action. They'll hear a bark and they'll respond to it. I use a bark most of the time simply to hold their attention. Often when there's aggressive barking going on, a squirrel's nature is to get out – climb out – where they can see. And many times, they'll bark back in response, even though they don't see the danger. They'll often bark simply to tell other squirrels that they have something pinpointed. So I'll use calls to either hold their attention or give away their location.

Me: Some folks – me, for instance – are familiar with the calls intended to reproduce the squirrel's bark. But there's another call, another sound, that's available, a high-pitched whistle meant to imitate the frantic sounds of a squirrel in distress. Tell me about that.

Harris: That distress call is phenomenal. As far as a success rate is concerned, there's no doubt that that call is the most successful when it comes to squirrels and squirrel hunting. And the reason it works so well is because squirrels are very protective. They're very aggressive. That distress call simulates a young squirrel being attacked by a hawk or an owl, and when that distress call is made – coupled with a little bit of limb shaking to simulate an owl knocking a squirrel off a limb – boy, they get real aggressive. And they respond by barking excitedly. This aggressive barking is meant, I think, to intimidate the predator, as well as to rally the other squirrels to come in out of a protective instinct. They're very aggressive to the (distress) sound, and they respond well to it.

Me: Is there a *best* time to use the distress style call?

Again, the blaze orange issue. To me, it's a no-brainer.

Harris: Anytime there's leaf cover. It works great early in the season when there's a lot of young squirrels out there – young ones that are being subjected to these various predators. But it works well throughout the year simply because the instinct to respond to the distress call of a young squirrel is so strong. What the leaf cover does is force the squirrels to come closer just to identify the source of the sound. They have to get closer to see what's going on. Once the leaf cover's gone, they'll jump up on a limb to take a look, but they can see so much farther and better that often they won't commit.

Me: Fox squirrels or gray squirrels? Which one responds to a call better? Or is there a difference?

Harris: I think the reds (fox squirrels) are more aggressive and more vulnerable to the call than the grays. Now I've had great days on the gray squirrels, but percentage-wise, fox squirrels seem a little more aggressive and respond a little better to the calls.

What is the future of squirrel hunting? My Pop, shown here with an Ohio gray, certainly hopes that small game hunting doesn't "get lost in the shuffle."

Me: You're in the call manufacturing and promotion business, Brad. Why isn't there more interest in squirrel calls and calling?

Harris: The biggest reason is on the promotion side of it. We just haven't done a good job of promoting squirrel calls. Back in the 1980s, Michael Pearce did a series of squirrel hunting articles. One of these was in Outdoor Life, and several other major outdoor magazines. Automatically, you could see the sales of squirrel calls skyrocket. And automatically you would start talking to people who had had success with it 'cause they had read about squirrel calls and it was something that they would go out and try. Squirrel calling just doesn't have the prestige like calling turkeys or calling elk or calling deer. It's a squirrel. I mean people just don't see calling squirrels as a tried and proven tactic, and they're totally wrong. It's a practice that just hasn't been publicized and passed down, as it should have been.

So there's another little something that we can use. I would like to say this before I continue. Sort of a combination of what my Pop and Harris had to say about the use of squirrel calls. While calls can be effective tools, they also add that extra aural element to the hunting situation. That is, maybe that other hunter saw your hand move as you reached for the call that was in your pocket. Thirty seconds later, he hears what he's sure is a fox squirrel barking. There's a flicker of movement at the base of a tree 40 yards away. A gun's raised. He's sure he sees a tail. Then a body. He pushes the safety off…

Melodramatic? Perhaps. But I'm sure you can see *exactly* where I'm going here. Is there a solution to the events just described? Well, first and foremost, there's prevention. This is a clear-cut case of target identification. The shooter didn't see a squirrel; he *thought* he saw a squirrel. Secondly, and here's where my Pop comes into play, there's the blaze orange issue. Personally, I've never had an instance where I can honestly say that I lost an opportunity to shoot a squirrel because that squirrel saw my blaze orange and ran away. However, there have been times when I've had other hunters tell me that they could see my blaze orange ball cap from 100 yards away. Why, they asked, would you where blaze orange when you're squirrel hunting? Truth is, with their "100-yard" comment, they'd answered their own question. 'Nough said. Let's get back to my Old Man and the tactics.

Me: Let's say you hear a squirrel barking. You know, generally speaking, where he is. What's your next move?

Pop: A barking gray squirrel? As soon as you move and he sees you, he's going to run. And if you're any distance from him, he's going to be gone long before you get anywhere close. Unless he's close and shootable at that time, you're kind of in a no-win situation with a gray or a black. Now with a fox squirrel, occasionally you'll be able to pick him out and approach him to within easy shooting distance. But a gray or a black, forget it. If he's shootable, you're set. If he's not shootable, it's best to just watch where he goes. Watch what he does. If you try to move on a gray, he's going to see you and he's going to run. That's it.

Me: I've heard you mention something unusual, something to the effect that squirrels – or at least those in your part of the country – are changing their habits. What do you mean by that?

Pop: It might be heresy to say this, but I've noticed over the past, maybe, five, six, seven years, squirrel hunting has seemed to become increasingly easier. I don't think squirrels are as afraid of humans as they used to be. Especially in woods that aren't hunted much. More and more, we're seeing fewer and fewer squirrel hunters. Except for the first couple weeks of the season, the rest of squirrel season is practically devoid of hunters. And I don't think that the squirrel population in any given area is hunted enough to make them people-shy. I've never seen the number of squirrels – like this past year – where you could be casually walking through the woods, maybe on the way back to the truck, and you happen to look up and there's a squirrel sitting on a limb, or on a trunk, or on the ground. Just sitting watching you, and making no attempt whatsoever to hide. I'm just not sure what that is.

Me: And finally, Pop, what's your take on the future of squirrel hunting in this country? Or is there a future?

Pop: I think we're running out of the generation that started out hunting squirrels. I was born in 1940 and when I was younger we hunted everything. We hunted rabbits, squirrels. Ducks weren't on our list, and I didn't hunt 'em simply because my Dad didn't. We hunted a little deer. And turkeys? At that time, there were no turkeys in Ohio. But small game and deer, we hunted it all. I think the present generation grew up with fathers who were species-specific hunters. Maybe it's due to time limitations. They work, and they only have so much vacation. They went to deer camp. Small game hunting became, more or less, a lost art. Take, for example, beagle men around home. I can count the number of beagle men around home these days on one hand. If they're taking the time to hunt today, it's the big stuff, or the glamour stuff. They'll hunt geese. They'll hunt turkeys. They'll hunt deer. They'll take a week's vacation and hunt deer. But in the meantime, small game has gotten lost in the shuffle.

My Pop, Mick, and Jeb, the beagle. The Old Man cleaned a lot of rabbits, and does to this day.

2

Fast Feet – Rabbits & Hares

*To me, it's not the size of the dog that matters.
It's the size of the dog's heart.
~ Brad Harris*

You always hit the eggs-and-toast diner first.

"Rabbit huntin'?" comes the fry cook's question.

You are indeed. Deer and wild turkey seasons have just ended and the so-called "second season" is arriving right on time. An eager beagle in the truck box says as much. The New Year might be coming soon, but this is the fresh start you've been waiting for.

Coffee in big foam cups to go. White fields. A dusting of snow. Multiflora rose thickets, and the full cry of that little hound await you. Cottontails lurk near ground holes, resting in their sun-warmed "forms." These shallow depressions are like mini-whitetail beds. The beagle gets a rabbit moving, following the scent trail, pushing the bunny in its inevitable tight circle, back to where shotguns wait. Only your eyes move as you await the approach. The cottontail freezes on the way in, studies your position, then bolts—"One coming your way," you shout. The dog follows moments after, and if you're a rabbit hunter, you smile. Life is good.

Shooting is clearly not all of it. But shots come, one there, then two more. "Got 'm."

The morning passes into noon. A tailgate lunch reveals the following in your orange game bag: a brace of cottontails, a bonus ringneck, bright as a Christmas package, and several more excuses regarding misses.

The afternoon winter glare finds you reaching for sunglasses. You sit down, taking a breather. This moment is a time of reflection. The folks you hunt with are close friends, family. Such times blend into seasonal reflections. Hunts in coverts old and new, with fresh bunny tracks offer hope you'll make game.

Forget New Age stuff. You want real aromatherapy? Try the smell of gunpowder on a winter rabbit hunt.

Steve Hickoff - good friend, full-time outdoor writer, and obvious devotee of one of our most traditional sporting pastimes — rabbit hunting.

Rabbit hunting's tailor-made for one and all. Here, Julie lofts a fine Iowa bunny taken during a December outing.

It was exciting waiting around for the calendar to read the November 15. Young and old anticipated the opener's arrival with the same enthusiasm as one might await Christmas. You see, everyone hunted rabbits back then. It was just something you did. It was something that *families* did. With everyone clad in well-rumpled canvas – perhaps a pair of too-big boots on the youngest member of the party. The image was made complete with a little tri-color beagle dog straining at a chewed leather lead.

Ah, yes. Those were the days. But I won't take the time here to talk about the tradition or the nostalgia. Or, for that matter, the fact that an alarmingly few people today chase rabbits with the dedication and the passion like that of the beaglemen of days gone by. No, that will all be addressed farther back in a piece I called *Where have all the rabbit hunters gone?*

Here, we're just going to talk about rabbits. And beagles, too. And brushpiles. Oh, and maybe a jackrabbit and a snowshoe hare, just for good measure. And let's not forget the most important thing when it comes to chasing bunnies: The fun. Lots of fun.

Meet the players

Every hunter knows that it doesn't take much to create a situation where there's a lot of rabbits. I mean, bunnies didn't come by their prolific reputation just because, now did they? But while a lot of rabbits – individuals units, that is – in any given location might not come as a surprise, it may shock some folks to learn there are over a dozen species and more than 70 subspecies of rabbits inhabiting the planet. That's rabbits now; not jackrabbits and snowshoes, both of which are hares and both of which will be discussed here in a bit. No, I'm talking just rabbits.

But despite the varieties – all these species and subspecies and such – hunters in the United States are going to encounter only a very small handful of these throughout their hunting careers. For many the likelihood is great that there will be but *one* rabbit in our lives – the cottontail.

The Eastern cottontail – I'm going to go out on a limb here and define the Eastern cottontail as the rabbit we're all familiar with; that is, except for the Alaskans, but they have rabbit-like critters of their own. Traditionally, the Eastern cottontail made its home from the Eastern Shore to the Plains States and everywhere in-between; however, cottontails have at one time or another been introduced into just about every corner of the continental United States. Today, it's tough to find a place lacking good numbers of bunnies. As an interesting note, the genus into which the Eastern cottontail is classified, *Sylvilagus*, translates into the Latin, *sylva*, meaning forest, and the Greek, *lagos*, meaning hare. Forest hare….get it?

I can't think of a time when I was growing up that we didn't hunt rabbits. For that matter, I can't remember a year when we didn't have a beagle. Oh, there were those seasons when we had good beagles, and there were those when we had great beagles; still, the bottom line was that come November 15, we hunted rabbits. That's all there was to it.

As for November 15, years ago that was THE day– opening day of rabbit season. Only when the 15th rolled around on a Sunday, a day that until recently was set aside strictly for church and football, did opening day change to the 16th. And the hour? Nine o'clock. Yes, things were simpler then. Opening day was the 15th, and the hours were from 9 a.m. until 5 p.m. There was none of this rotating opener or first Saturday following the first full moon in November kind of thing. Shooting hours were not one half hour before sunrise to sunset. Nope, it was 9 'til 5. Some folks know them as bankers' hours. We knew them as rabbit season.

The eastern cottontail, well known across most of the United States.

Swamp rabbits and cane-cutters – Both swamp rabbits (*Sylvilagus aquaticus*) and marsh rabbits (*Sylvilagus palustris*) are technically cottontails; however, there are some differences. These are large animals. The males can weigh upwards of 5 to 6 pounds. Swamp rabbits are perhaps better known as cane-cutters because of the way they snip their favorite food. These particular rabbits inhabit a large area of the south-central United States, where they frequent low-lying timbered wetland areas and soggy thickets. Another Southerner, the marsh rabbit is partial to portions of Virginia, Georgia, Florida, and Alabama, where, like its cousin the cane-cutter, it makes its home in the soggy bottoms and thickets.

Western rabbits – When I moved to Washington in 1993, I soon discovered that Eastern cottontails weren't only an "Eastern" thing. Washington has a ton of cottontails. It's also home to the tiny pygmy rabbit, a very uncommon shirttail relation to the Eastern cottontail, and the subject of much controversial funding and research in The Evergreen State. Pygmy rabbits aren't hunted in Washington; cottontails are. Other Western bunnies include the brush rabbit of Oregon and California, and the desert cottontail, a slightly larger cottontail look-alike found from the central Rockies down into portions of the American Southwest.

Rabbit senses and, defenses

If you've ever watched any documentary show about Africa, chances are you've seen wildebeests. Well, regardless of what the show is actually about and regardless of the role the wildebeests actually play, it doesn't take long before you notice a common thread linking all of these programs – everything in Africa eats wildebeest. From crocodiles to lions, leopards and to hyenas, all the predators go after the wildebeest. That's just the way it is when you're a wildebeest.

I mention the wildebeest for one reason; cottontails are the North American equivalent of the wildebeest. Everything loves bunnies. Coyotes, foxes, hawks and owls all relish a rabbit dinner. 'Coon and skunks take the little ones. Dogs and feral cats, bobcats and golden eagles, not to mention any number of falcons and the occasional lynx all hunt rabbits. And wolves…can't forget them. Last but certainly not least is the human element.

So what's this all mean? Are we soon destined to be a world without rabbits? No, rabbits aren't without their ways and means of keeping the coyotes and the red-tails at a safe distance. Or rather, keeping themselves a safe distance from the fangs and talons that would dearly love a plump little bunny.

Better to see you with – Look closely at a rabbit, and

Speed, agility, hearing, and vision - he's got it all. And while he may look soft and fuzzy, the cottontail is far from defenseless.

tontail's ears help funnel sound waves into the inner ear – a task they accomplish quite well. The long ears also help to dissipate heat during the warmer months.

You don't see me – Typically, the conversation would go something like this.

> **Dad:** He's right there. See him?
> **Me:** Where?
> **Dad:** Right there, beside that clump of weeds. See him?
> **Me:** Where?
> **Dad:** Follow my finger. He's right there in the open.
> **Me:** I still don't see him. Where?
> **Dad:** Here, look down the rib of the gun right over the bead.
> **Me:** Wait. I…I still don't see him. Where is he?
> **Dad:** (Big sigh) Watch. (The Old Man takes two steps, and the rabbit runs off.)

Just what is it about fathers that allow them to see rabbits the rest of us can't see? Personally, I think it's biological. Or comes with age. Anyway, I mention the above exchange to spotlight one of the cottontail's favorite lines of defense – doing nothing. Squatting low and remaining motionless has saved more than one bunny's hide from a prowling red-tail or ambling shotgunner. The ability to sit still is thanks in part to nerves that would rival those of a rooster pheasant, and natural camouflage that's second to none. I've always been told to "look for the rabbit's eye." While the cottontail's brownish-gray color blends perfectly with many types of cover, there's really nothing he can do to hide that shiny marble of an eye. I just hope they never learn to squint.

Run away! – See it once and you'll understand the truth in the old saying, "Running like a scared rabbit." No slouches when it comes to speed, cottontails are quite adept at using those long hind legs to put distance between themselves and a potential threat. While bunnies, like roosters or ruffed grouse, seem to be moving at the speed of sound, the Good Lord has yet to build a rabbit that can outrun even a standard field load of #6 shot. Sure, he looks like he's fast – and he is! The trick is to take your time and not get flustered.

Strength in numbers – Again, there's truth in the adage, "Multiplying like rabbits." I've read that just two adult cottontails, given ideal conditions, can potentially grow into a population of 350,000 in just five years. That's a lot of bunny rabbits! Certainly, such ideal conditions don't exist, as there will always be the mortality factor; however, the example does show that the cottontail's machine-gun birth rate, like its legs, ears, and eyes, is just

you'll notice that rabbits have big eyes. You'll also notice that these big bulging orbs are situated not in front of the rabbit's face, but rather on the sides of its head. Eyes this size gather an immense amount of light and allow the rabbit to see well in low-light situations when he's most active – dawn, dusk, and at night. This helps protect him from day predators, but what about the night hunters like coyotes and owls? Well, these light-gathering eyes are incredibly sharp; what's more, they can sense even the slightest movement, and all motion, at least to a cottontail, translates into RUN AWAY or hide. The positioning of a rabbit's eyes afford him an incredible field of vision. That is to say a bunny can see all but about 80 degrees or so directly behind his head. All of this visual information not only helps keep rabbits safe from predators, but explains exactly how and why that cottontail ran when all you did was "raise your gun." I've been there…done that one.

Better to hear you with – One look at a cottontail's ears, and it's obvious they're not there for decoration. Like the whitetail's ears or the barn owl's facial disk, the cot-

A South Dakota jackrabbit doing what he does best - running.

one of the many things designed to ensure continuing populations of these fascinating game animals.

Outdoor writer, Patrick McManus, writes of two kinds of what he calls kid camping – one is *camping with*, and the other is *camping without*. For those of you who read, reminisced, and laughed at the story, you already know the difference. Those of you who haven't had the pleasure, the difference is simple. *Camping with* means camping outside **with** a buddy, while *camping without*…well, you see where this is going.

I mention McManus' outdoor explanations for a reason. Rabbit hunting is done with and without. As you'll soon see, as it applies to bunnies, *with* and *without* has absolutely nothing to do with a hunting partner. A **human** hunting partner, that is.

Rabbit hunting with…

Looking back now, I guess there were lots of things I didn't realize. Who knew some kids actually went to school on the opening day of duck season? Did you realize there were folks who liked to **catch** crappies but didn't like to eat them? I'm still shaking my head about that one. But did you also realize there are those who hunt rabbits without a beagle dog?

For years, I was convinced that somewhere in the Ohio hunting regulations, there was a statement that said something to the effect that all hunters pursuing cottontails must, with no exceptions, possess and use a tri-colored hound of the beagle variety. As far as I was concerned,

My Pop, Mick, and one of his many beagle dogs, Jeb. It was hard to decide who enjoyed chasing bunnies better.

A pack of sharp-nosed beagles and a couple of good friends provide the primary ingredients for a most excellent afternoon afield.

the beagle statute was law, like Thanksgiving in November and Christmas in December. Beagle dogs were an integral part of the rabbit hunting process when I grew up. And rabbit hunting *with*...well, that was just the way it was.

Today, and compared to the early 1970s when I was chasing cottontails in northeast Ohio, relatively few folks chase rabbits at all; however, many of those who do still believe in this "gotta have a beagle" rule.

"It's like taking your sister to the prom," an old Trumbull County rabbit chaser once told me when I asked him about the concept of hunting without a dog. "Sure, you got a date, but people are gonna look at you funny." That's perhaps an odd way to phrase it, but he certainly left no doubt as to what he was talking about.

Back in the spring of 2001, Julie and I had the opportunity to share some time in the Missouri woods with a man who loves nothing more than spending a morning walking behind a pack of hollering beagles. Recognized perhaps more for his prowess with a turkey call, Brad Harris, Lohman Game Calls' chief public relations man, is also one of the most dedicated beaglers to ever leash a black-and-white-and-tan. In speaking with him, Brad's enthusiasm for what many believe to be almost a lost art is contagious. Even over the telephone, you can hear the excitement in his voice when he talks about training new puppies or watching a kid kill his first cottontail. In person? Well, you'd just have to experience that enthusiasm for yourself!

In between early morning wake-ups that spring, I asked Brad to talk a bit about rabbits and beagles – the intricacies, if you will, about the hound-hunting process, and for that matter, why is that beagles and bunnies go so very well together. I don't think you'll read far before you see the same passion that we did. And with that, I give you the alliterative offering –

Beagle, bunnies, and Brad Harris

Me: Okay, Brad. Just what is it about rabbit hunting with beagles that you find so exciting?

Harris: To me, it's the thrill of the chase. To me, watching dogs is outstanding 'cause you see the love and the desire and the passion in them for what it is they're bred to do. To hear the sound, the music, the barking, or the harking as they used to call it in the old circles. It's just beautiful music to me to listen to these beagles when they're on the trail. The energy they exert trying to find the rabbit. And it's also tradition. I mean, hunting dogs and rabbit hunting is just an outstanding tradition that I wouldn't want to see die. And you just have to be out there and live it in order to understand it.

Me: Technical question here – Which is the better rabbit hound, male or female?

Harris: I'm middle of the road there. You could poll

100 different beaglers and you'd get 100 different answers. My best all-around beagle was a female. You couldn't ask for a better dog in every respect. And yet the best dog in my kennel right now is a male. Best dog meaning he does the job for me in the field and does it right in a classic style. So I've had good dogs, both male and female, so I'm not going to sweat the sex issue. I'm not going to let it distract me from finding the right beagle dog. Male or female – I think the biggest factor is the 'in heat' factor with the females and the breeding instincts. And that's the key. If you don't want to worry about pups and you don't want to worry about putting her up during her cycle, I would suggest you go with a male. But for me? I'm looking for the classic beagle, and I don't care what sex or color it is.

Me: Picking a pup can be an awful tough decision. Any advice there?

Harris: This is a personal answer, and there'll be 1,000 guys agree and disagree with me on this. I think that's part of you as a houndsman. That's a part of your own inner feeling. What gives you the feeling of a classic hunt or a classic dog. Things I look for when I'm looking for puppies? Right off the bat, I'm looking for curiosity and adventuring. I want a pup that's busy and looking. It's nosy and energetic. To me, I feel like those things might give them an edge in the field. So I'm looking for a pup that's not shy. That's bold. And that starts in them right as a pup. You know, the one that gets away from Mama the farthest. It's always out and alert. Maybe something 200 yards from the kennel gets its attention. Those are the things that I'm looking for in a pup. As far as the size? I've had 15-inch beagles that were outstanding, and I've had 12-inch and miniature beagles that were outstanding. To me, it's not the size of the dog that matters. It's the size of the dog's heart.

Me: Where do you find these puppies, Brad? The newspaper? Or maybe a kennel? Or someone who specializes in raising beagles?

Harris: I've have friends who have kennels and have raised beagles for 30 years. These guys, it's said, have never had a bad dog in 30 years. And by going to these folks who have had this kind of longevity and this kind of reputation, the chance that you're going to find a fine hound is going to go up. Now there's no guarantee in dogs. In the same respect, the breeding of this beagle and this beagle and this housedog beagle that's never seen a rabbit doesn't mean they won't be rabbit dogs? They just might be the best rabbit dog you've ever seen, but the percentages aren't in your favor. You wanna go after the percentages, those dogs that, generation after generation, have become quality dogs; still there's no guarantee to it.

Me: Formal training for beagles? I mean, the same type of training that you might expect to find given a pointer or a field trial retriever?

Harris: As far as formal training for a rabbit dog, there's really not such a thing. The key is them knowing

Running a young dog with an older, experienced hound can be a good thing; however, Harris cautions against the possibility of transferring bad habits.

their name. And then coming and knowing you're the man that when you call them, they come. They don't run off-game, and they learn to hunt with you. That they're not independent and leaving the pack and leaving you to hunt on their own. Other than those common obedience things, there's really no formal training. It's just a matter of time and giving them ample time to learn the tricks of the trade in the field running the rabbits.

Some beagles are slower starters than others, and you have to be careful with that. I've seen pups that were extremely fast starters, and by four or five months, they're doing some really good stuff. And the litter in the next kennel over, they're not even ready to start at four and five months. But, two years down the road, you look at the slow starters and they're much better dogs than the ones that got off with such a big bang. So, yes, I do believe the desire to hunt is bred into beagles. If they have the proper lineage, they are going to be hunters. That doesn't mean they're going to be great dogs, but they'll have the desire to go out and hunt. The key is giving them time to develop 'cause they don't all develop at the same age.

Me: When do you start introducing your beagle pups to the concept of gunfire?

Harris: That starts out at two and three weeks old. Not firing guns over them, but for the first few weeks of their lives, I'm not quiet around my beagle pups. When I go out to feed, I bang the water pans together. I bang the

31

A hot bunny track and a pat on the head after the fact are all a beagle dog needs. Oh, and a bite of Moon Pie from time to time.

Harris: I don't do it the first few times out, depending on the dog. The first few times in the field, I want that dog to go and be adventurous. You stay with them. I just don't turn 'em out. I stay with them 'cause when I'm out hunting, I want them to know that they're hunting with me. And that starts with the pups. So when I take two or three pups out at a time, I'm right there with them. I'm encouraging them to look. I'm talking to them. I want them to realize that this is a partnership. They're with me and I'm with them. I'm not going to leave them and they're not going to leave me. This is when you'll see those pups that will get out there 30 or 40 yards and be sticking their nose in every brush pile. They don't know exactly what they're looking for, but they're looking. Until they know what they're looking for, I'll take them out on their own or with other puppies – and keep a very, very close eye on 'em.

Many times if you put a pup out with an experienced dog, they don't learn anything but hitchhiking. They'll just follow the old dog and run with it. Yes, they'll eventually learn to run, but they don't form any independence in that respect. Once they learn what the rabbit is and they start showing some promise, then I may introduce an older dog to help 'em get finished out.

Me: To back up a bit. So you say there's no real formal training? Is there anything that you feel **must** be instilled in these pups in order for them to be effective in the field?

Harris: These pups need to know what "no" means. You start than in the kennel at an early age. Take excess barking. I'll turn the hose on 'em. I have a beagle right now – call him Rowdy 'cause he's rowdy – and he's gonna be something. But right now, that dog is a barking fool in the kennel. I use the water hose. Just give him a squirt and tell him "no!" whenever I want him to shut up. Or if I catch him digging. Or if I catch him doing something I don't want him doing. I give him a squirt with the water hose and tell him "no!" And I guarantee you that when I tell him "no!" now, he knows. I have not hit him. But I can walk out now when he's barking and tell him "no!" and he'll shut up. It's important that you establish all of the loving and "come here" and the praise at a young age, but you also have to establish the "no!" This way when you get into the field and they hit that deer or opossum or armadillo and you say "no!" they know it's wrong.

Me: Julie's black lab, Jet, will retrieve rabbits, but I've never personally owned a beagle that would retrieve rabbits. Have you?

Harris: I've had two or three beagles over the years that would retrieve rabbits. Rather, I'd allow them to retrieve rabbits. I have one in my kennel right now that if you shoot a rabbit in the brush, it disappears in the briars and when he finds that rabbit dead, he'll bring it back and lay it at your feet. It's awesome. Some dogs have that natural trait. It's really not something that you can train into

food pans together. From the time they're just crawling around in the box, when they hear me coming, they're hearing my voice talking to the female or talking to the other beagles in the kennel. And I'm whistling and making noise. They get accustomed to loud noises. And I think that's very important. If you go out there and you're very quiet and you don't make any noise when you feed them, well those dogs get pretty peaceable. What I want to do is to introduce those dogs to loud sounds. Sure, it'll startle them from time to time, but then they hear my voice calming them and talking to the other dogs, and real soon they're not paying any attention to that water pan being slammed against the gatepost.

Once I start running them in the field, sometimes I'll use a starter's pistol, often just when the chase gets started and they're barking and they're excited. But I always make sure that they're intrigued and involved in the chase. I pick my times carefully to fire my pistol. Sometimes I'll wait until the pups are 20 or 30 yards off in the brush, and I'll fire a shot in the air. Have 'em come running to me. Now that shot might have startled 'em, but they hear my voice and they come running in and I'm petting 'em and everything's fine. We're all having fun. It's a slow process, and you have to pick your times when to introduce them to that shot. But only rarely will you find a dog that you can't train properly as far as the gun's concerned.

Me: I've always been told, Brad, that it's a good idea to run a young dog with an older, more experienced beagle to show them the ropes. Your thoughts on that one?

a beagle, and many times, I discourage my dogs from taking the rabbit from the spot where I shoot it. I don't want it to go from there. I don't mind them mouthing it – that's their reward – but I won't allow tug-of-wars or pick it up and take off with it. That's a no-no, and I will never tolerate that. But as for retrieving, it's just a special dog that does that. There are some that do it, and it's nice as long as it doesn't create a big fight or a big tug-of-war between him and rest of the dogs.

Me: Growing up, we always used to field-dress our rabbits and still do today. Plus, we used to give some of the innards – the heart and lungs and liver – to the beagles as a treat. What's you're take on this practice?

Harris: I do that *all* the time. I believe in field-dressing your rabbits. I think it makes for better table fare and it's just proper game care. I carry a pocketknife with me, and every rabbit you shoot, you stand there and you field dress that rabbit. I pick the rabbit up, field dress it, and divvy up the heart-lung area to the dogs. It's just a reward and a nice treat for them. It slows down the hunt, the action, and gives you a little time to reflect on what happened.

Let me take just a second here and talk about tularemia, or *rabbit fever* as it's sometimes called. Tularemia is caused by and transmitted from host to host by biting insects – fleas and ticks being two of the most common carriers – and is known to be 100 percent fatal in those cottontails that it afflicts. It is not, however, fatal to humans, responding well to a number of different antibiotics. In truth, modern instances of rabbit-transmitted tularemia are few and far between, perhaps because infected cottontails quickly succumb to the virus and thus are eliminated from the contagion equation. Some sources suggest that hunters who opt to field-dress their rabbits should wear rubber gloves during the process. We never did, and don't today, and I have yet to come down with what I thought was a case of rabbit fever; however, if rubber gloves give you a sense of calm, then by all means carry a pair in your rabbit hunting coat. Oh, and by the way. If you're concerned about the possibility of contracting tularemia yourself by eating wild rabbit, don't worry; that is, unless you're eating raw rabbit sushi, in which case you probably deserve tularemia.

A couple other things before we get back to Harris, these about rabbits, innards, and dogs. First, damn near all rabbits have tapeworms, which can be passed along to your beagle **if** the dog is given innards other than the heart, liver, and lungs. Because of this, we always hung the innards in a nearby tree after we field-dressed the rabbit. Neglect this step, and I can guarantee that your beagle will be "lost" for a few minutes once the hunt resumes, only to return smacking its little beagle lips. Beagles love rabbit guts. That's just the way it is.

The second word of caution concerns livers with little white spots. This goes back to the aforementioned tularemia, the white spots on the liver being a recognized symptom of the disease. Outward signs that a rabbit might be infected include a sluggish or almost tame behavior – a reluctance to run, staggering and that sort of thing. Regardless, feeding white-spotted livers to your hound probably isn't a good idea; however, and again, such rabbits are fit for human consumption as long as they're thoroughly cooked.

And now, back to Brad -

Me: What is it, Brad, about beagles and bunnies and kids? That they just seem to go together?

Harris: There *is* a tie between kids, beagles, and bunnies. To me, kids and beagles are a whole lot alike. They're fun loving, carefree. They like to please you. You know, kids, when they're young, they like to make Mom and Dad happy. Kids want to make you happy, and most hunting dogs want to please their master. They just blend so well. And how the rabbit comes into play with those two is that it's an enjoyable time to be afield, and it creates a lot of action. I mean, the barking and the chasing, and the kids love that action.

Me: Let's say someone's new to rabbit hunting behind beagles. Are there any instructions that you give this person before or during their first outing with you and your hounds?

Harris: First and foremost, I let people know right up front that those dogs are very important to me. They're like my kids. I just love 'em to death. They're out here and they're working hard, and all they know is the hunt. They don't know to watch you, so you have to watch them. Secondly, I don't allow jump-shooting of rabbits when I'm hunting with the dogs. I don't allow .22 rifles when I'm hunting over dogs with novice rabbit hunters. I allow 20-gauge or .410 shotguns, and we don't jump-shoot rabbits. So the only rabbit you shoot is the rabbit that those dogs are running. What I go for is to listen to these dogs run. I go for the race, not for the rabbit killing. So we'll jump a rabbit, position everyone safely so you know where everyone's at, and take the dogs over to the track. You realize that you have a pack of dogs after that rabbit, and that you have to positively identify that rabbit. Where your shot's going and where those dogs are at all times.

This is especially true with young dogs. With young dogs, sometimes one will get tired and break from the race and come back. So expect to see a young dog instead of a rabbit. So it's gun safety and it's education, and it's up to the dog owner to educate the people he's with and keep control of the situation.

At this point, I'd like to add a note about why rabbit hunting *with* works the way it does. You see, bounced out of their beds, cottontails that don't run in

Taking an elevated stand like this hunter has done can provide a much better vantage point.

a razor-straight line for their holes have a tendency to run in a circle. Sometimes it's a big circle, and other times, it's a smaller circle. Regardless of the circumference of said rabbit circle, it's a habit, and one that houndsmen have capitalized on for generations. Basically, the entire process happens like this –

1. The rabbit is flushed from hiding, either by a size 12 boot or the cold, wet nose of an inquisitive beagle dog.

2. The same rabbit runs while the hound or hounds pursue. It's interesting to note here that more often than not, the cottontails take a pretty leisurely approach to this run-and-chase thing. Oh, he'll get 50 yards or so ahead of the dogs, and then he'll go to nibbling on a wild rose bush or scratching behind his head with a hind leg. Every now and then, he'll stop whatever it is he's doing and raise his head for an update. Once the dogs close the gap to the point that the rabbit feels pressured, he'll run another 50 yards, stop, and commence nibbling again. All in all, it's pretty comical.

3. While the hounds are in hot pursuit, you, the hunter, take a stand not too far from where the rabbit was jumped. Chances are his circle will bring him back through this general area. I'm not sure why it happens this way. I only know that it does. Standers would do well to remain motionless and watch using only their eyes until time to shoot.

And rabbit hunting without –

I'd be lying if I said I haven't spent many a morning rabbit hunting *without*; that is, sans beagle dogs. Once my father's beagle, Jeb, passed away in the mid-1990s, and I moved from Ohio to the Pacific Northwest, I never really had the opportunity to get behind a beagle or two in the field; however, that didn't mean that I quit rabbit hunting all together. I've done quite a bit of rabbit chasing in the years since that last beagle dog.

While I certainly do miss the yips and howls of a Nellie or a Missy or a Spike-dog hot on the trail of a cottontail, I do enjoy rabbit hunting without. I have had to change my methods a bit since going hound-less; however, there's still nothing at all high-tech nor equipment intensive about those strategies which I'll call *walking* and *stalking*.

Walking them up

There's probably not a farm kid in the country that hasn't walked at least one bunny out of an old fenceline and rolled him with his trusty Model 870 Wingmaster. And that's really all there is to the tactic known as walk-

ing them up. Essentially, you put yourself in rabbit country, and you walk until you flush a rabbit. Sometimes, the cottontails will be sunning themselves in the short brome grass on a southern exposure. Other days, they'll all be hunkered into the thickest clumps of downfall and multi-flora rose in the section. Some of the most enjoyable – and the most exciting –hunts I've had have come after a heavy snow. Under these conditions, I'll find a set of rabbit tracks that meander away from the cover. Eventually, these tracks will disappear into a small frost-lined hole in the snow – the rabbit's nest for the day. Often, you'll have to stomp a section of ground the size of a 1975 Olds Delta 98 before the bunny explodes like a Bouncing Betty, snow flying every which way. Just try to hit that one. As I mentioned earlier, there's really no trick to it; however, I will take a couple minutes and speak briefly about arms and ammunition, as well as a handful of safety reminders.

As far as guns and ammo are concerned, it's tough to make a poor choice when it comes to cottontails. Sure, some folks will argue that the .410, with its $^{11}/_{16}$ ounce of shot leaves hunters a bit under-gunned; still, I'm somewhat partial to the little gun, when, that is, it's used within its limitations of both range and pattern. Typically, though, when you find me in the field chasing bunnies, I'll have with me either a 20-gauge or one of my favorite 16s. Both offer more than adequate 1-ounce loads. Neither is so heavy as to make the transition from shotgun to cinder block by day's end. The 12-gauge? Certainly, the 12 is not *too* much gun for rabbits; however, I find quite a few of them a bit weighty and cumbersome to carry all day. Too, if you're going to shoot 1-ounce shotshells, why not opt for the same load in a lighter, faster-swinging 20 or 16?

And as for the shot sizes – well, I'm a fan of #6 shot from season start to season finish. Thin-skinned and relatively light-boned, cottontails aren't difficult to kill; however, the brush and cover that they frequent does do a fantastic job of absorbing shotshell patterns. And those pellets that bury themselves in a sumac aren't going to do me much good, now are they? With this in mind, I settled on #6s due to the high pellet count and excellent pattern density that comes with the 1-ounce loads. For those of you with an extra box of #7½ shot sitting around, by all means use it. I do like #7½ shot for my rabbit hunting, just exactly for the reasons stated above; however, I won't go any smaller simply because I don't want to be picking through 300 #8 pellets during my next rabbit pot pie.

It doesn't matter what the game species, safety is always – ALWAYS – of the utmost concern. With cottontails, the most significant safety issue I've encountered, and this one primarily for those hunting *without*, lies in the importance of always – ALWAYS – knowing exactly

The author, along with hunting partner, Darren Johnson, walked up this eastern Iowa cottontail during a winter hunt. Note the muzzleloading double, a fine rabbit gun.

where the other members of your hunting party are. When a bunny jumps unexpectedly, a whole lot of things happen in a very, very brief period of time. You see the rabbit and identify it as a rabbit, and not a groundhog, feral cat…I'll give you a break on the feral cat…or other non-game species. The gun goes up, the safety goes off, and you begin to establish your lead on the rapidly departing critter. Your finger reaches for the trigger. All of this happens in a fraction of a second. The question is, do you know where your partner is? For me, the answer is my requirement that all members of the hunting party wear (1) a blaze orange hat, and (2) at least some blaze orange on the chest or shoulders. I don't how many times I've raised a gun only to catch a flicker of blaze orange out of the corner of my eye. And the gun goes down. It's pretty elemental – blaze orange can help prevent accidents. It's works. Trust me.

The silent approach

I believe I could have subtitled this section – Spot & Stalk – and been just as accurate in my summation of the process, for that's precisely what this method entails. A

huge fan of rabbit hunting, my wife loves nothing more than slipping through a wintry woodlot or pastured timber, armed with her favorite Stevens .22/.410 over/under – iron sights no less – in hopes of catching a cottontail or two out for a brief laze in the sun. Or a bite of rose hips…whatever gets him out and away from cover for just a bit. Snow helps here, understandably, as an all-grey bunny stands out against an all-white background like a Styrofoam cup in a coal bin. Plus, the snow provides population information in the form of tracks, and thus armed with such information, Julie can concentrate her efforts on those areas that show the most activity. Remember, however, that one cottontail can in the course of an evening make an amazing number of tracks. So don't assume that a million tracks means a million bunnies. It might, but generally doesn't.

The perfect day to practice the silent approach, claims Julie, is a sunny day in December with three to four inches of new snow on the ground. Given such conditions, she'll generally start her search on the southern exposures, especially if the temperatures have slipped well below the freezing mark. Temperature, she says, doesn't seem to affect cottontails; not nearly as much, she believes, as does the presence or absence of sunshine. "Give a bunny a

Armed with her pet Savage .22/.410 O/U, Julie shares an after-hunt moment with her father-in-law.

place to sit in the sun, and he'll be there regardless of the thermometer," she says.

From here, it's not all together different than still-hunting whitetails. Move slowly and quietly, stopping frequently to visually pick the surrounding cover apart piece by piece. "Look for a rabbit part. Not the entire bunny," instructs my wife. "It's just like looking for a whitetail or blacktail in the timber. You're looking for an ear. Or an eye. Or the curve of the back. Something – some shape – that doesn't belong in the wild."

"This kind of hunting," she continues, "I think really helps teach you to become a better deer hunter. Perhaps even a better all-around hunter. It teaches you to slow down. It teaches you how to look for game. It teaches you how to move in the field. And with the .22, it helps improve your shooting skills. Plus, I dearly love to eat rabbit, so the end-result benefits for me are excellent."

A native of Washington state, Julie was raised around blacktails, Roosevelt elk, and centerfire rifles; hence, the reason she prefers the .22/.410 over/under for her late-winter rabbit hunting. She does, however, offer a trio of tips and reminders for those who would follow in her rimfire footsteps –

On open sights – "I prefer open sights, not because I want something that affords me the opportunity to take running shots more easily, but simply because that's what I grew up with. I'm more comfortable shooting open sights, and occasionally I'll get into low-light situations either in or on the edge of woodlots where the iron sights just seem to be more effective."

On scopes – "For deer, yes; for rabbits, no."

On bullet selection – "Basically, I'll use whatever my .22 shoots best; however, I do prefer a solid 40-grain bullet as opposed to a hollow point. Personal preference, I guess. Head shots only are my goal, and because of that, I guess it really wouldn't matter – solid or hollow point; still, my over/under likes the solids and I've had good luck with them in the past."

On favorite strategies – "If, for whatever reason, I can't find bunnies sitting out in the open, I'll go to the more traditional method of beating the brush. Often, rabbits will only run a short distance before they stop…kind of like a big mule deer buck stopping to look back at what disturbed him. When I jump a rabbit, I'll just get myself ready and try to be ready should he stop within, say, 50 yards or so. Too, I enjoy hunting in teams – one hunter with a shotgun, and me with my .22. Again, it goes back to the fact that some rabbits will stop and look back. That's when I get my chance."

A fresh snow and an old side-by-side muzzleloading shotgun make for excellent companions on this late-season hunt in eastern Iowa.

The snowshoe hare. An all-white rabbit against an all-brown background. Can you say 'styrofoam cup in a coal bin?'

On safety – "A lot of folks disagree with my choice of a .22 for rabbits, saying that these relatively slow solid bullets are a ricochet hazard, particularly on frozen ground. I can't argue that possibility; however, if you pick your shots carefully – and, yes, there will be some that you have to pass up for safety reasons – and never just open up on a running target, I really don't see any problem. Would I use a .22 in a large group? No, but then again, I see this type of hunting as a one-on-one or perhaps two-on-one type of thing."

Jackrabbits & hares

I'm going to go out on a limb here, and say that for every person in the Lower 48 who's familiar with some variety of hare, there's 100 – maybe 1,000 – who have some knowledge of rabbits. Especially cottontails. The reasons, I've learned, are both understandable as well as elemental. Cottontails, it seems, can be found just about everywhere, while hares have been scattered at random about the country. And while it wasn't always this way, today's modern outdoor chef would much rather roast a rabbit than put together a snowshoe stew or a varying hare gumbo. So there's the culinary aspect.

Still, and despite the fact that these big brothers to the bunnies aren't as well-known as their cotton-tailed cousins, they're certainly worthy of mention. In the United States, hunters may at one time or another encounter a handful of hares….sorry, I couldn't resist that one. These would include –

Snowshoe hares – Also known as varying hares, for the fact that their color *varies* from a dark brown in the spring and summer to pure white in the fall and winter. I shot my first snowshoe in western Washington in 2001, and was surprised at both the size of their well-furred feet and, once skinned, how incredibly skinny a creature they are. Nothing at all like the fat cottontails I grew up with in Ohio. Although snowshoes have been introduced into states such as Ohio, the hares make their homes primarily in Alaska, Canada, and the northern and mountain states of the Lower 48.

Hunting snowshoes, either *with* or *without*, remains quite the tradition in the New England states, as well as in parts of the Upper Midwest such as Michigan's Upper

Kevin Michalowski with the first white-tailed jackrabbit that Julie and I had ever seen up-close. Fine shooting, Mick.

Peninsula and the central and northern reaches of Wisconsin. The folks that I've spoken with, those that consider themselves avid or semi-avid snowshoe hunters, prefer the *with* method, the canine of choice being a small – surprise! – beagle dog; however, it is possible to hunt these northern hares in a the stomp-and-shoot technique more commonly associated with the hunting of cottontails. Stomping the brush, that is.

White-tailed & black-tailed jackrabbits – Let me just say this about jackrabbits. If what you're accustomed to are cottontails, jackrabbits are going to appear about the same size as a small goat. The first one I ever saw was in South Dakota, and upon retrieving my jaw from the dirt, I quickly determined that jackrabbits are about 45 percent ears, 45 per-

cent legs, and 10 percent something connecting the two. I learned later that the white-tailed jack, which I'd seen, inhabits the northern or north-central part of the country, while its cousin, the black-tailed jack, resides primarily in the West and south into Mexico. A third species, the antelope jackrabbit, can be found in Arizona and New Mexico.

For the most part, jackrabbits, when they are brought to ground by the shotgunner, are done so as incidentals. Such was the case in South Dakota during a November pheasant outing when our editor, Kevin Michalowski, bagged the white-tail pictured on this page. In most locales, however, jacks are the target of long-range centerfire enthusiasts, and can provide excellent opportunities for those with a passion for things well beyond 300 yards. Pistoleros, too, may want to get in on the action.

Gordy Krahn. In my mind, a master predator hunter, and the 'meal' that this winter coyote thought he heard.

3

The Villans – Predators & Varmints

Predator hunting gets into the blood. It replaces fighter T-cells, breaking down the immune system. In advanced stages, it weakens the mind and monopolizes rational thought. That's why many wives and girlfriends refer to it as a disease.

Passion for hiding in the undergrowth, imitating a fox's or coyote's supper, grows with every trip afield—æor whenever hunting compadres gather at local sporting goods stores or coffee shops to swap their sordid tales.

I was hooked early on, but didn't fully understand the full ramifications until years later. As I recall, it was an unusually warm September afternoon. With my trusty grouse gun tucked under one arm, I zigged and then zagged across a white birch ridge, hoping to put one of the flighty birds to wing.

A flash of silky red fur across the clearing triggered an age-old response. I quickly dropped to the ground and eased behind a moss-covered log, shotgun tucked close by my side. I peered over the log and watched a large male fox, oblivious to my presence; intently work the dry grass and fallen leaves for whatever groceries he could rustle up. I pursed my lips and emitted a soft squeak. Seconds later I heard his faint footfalls as the fox approached the log where I was hiding. I had no intention of shooting. Autumn was in its early stages and fur was far from prime. However, I had a strong hankering to trick the fabled trickster, and he was falling for the oldest ruse in the book.

I held my breath as the fox placed his front paws on the log and cautiously peered over the top, head cocked to one side. Our eyes locked and we both involuntarily jolted, uncomfortable with the abrupt invasion of personal space. The fox nearly turned himself inside out trying to put some ground between us, but suddenly slid to a stop, not 30 yards away. He turned around and gave me a lasting, sly look, as if to say, "You won't get me with that next time." Then he turned and melted into the golden forest.

The experience, more that 30 years ago in northern Minnesota, set the hook. And the thrill of that moment, and so many that followed over the years, transformed an otherwise "normal" sportsman into a predator-hunting fanatic. And now I'm betting that as you turn the following pages the hook will once again be set … that you will be inspired to dust off your hunting gear and take to the field for a glimpse of that elusive flash of fur!

Gordy Krahn, is the editor of *North American Hunter* magazine, and the gentleman in part responsible for my choosing freelance outdoor writing as a career choice. Thanks, Gordy. I owe you one.

A long-time fox hunter, the author shoulders a fine Iowa red taken on a December morning outing.

From hunter to hunted

My initiation into the art that is predator hunting wasn't altogether different from Gordy's. And yet it was. I don't know what it was that inspired my father and me to take up fox hunting. We didn't know anyone who did it. We had no mentors. No leaders. And no egomanical reason to want to do it. We knew little about foxes, other than they dined on rabbits, bobwhites, and occasionally the handful of wild pheasants that made Ohio their home in the early 1980s.

Looking back, our home-made caller – the 8-ohm car speaker wired inside an old cardboard cigar box, the dilapidated cassette player with the handle cut off so it would fit into our U.S. military surplus bag, and 30 feet of red-and-white wire – left a whole hell of a lot to be desired when compared with today's compact disc and digital players. But we didn't care. Why? Well, first, we didn't know any better. Secondly, high-tech in the predator-call-

ing realm back then meant a Burnham Brothers cassette player outfit, complete with the hard plastic case and the black locking closures. Now that was big time. And finally, why should we have cared? Our $1.98 Goodwill caller worked. Boy, howdy, did it work. It fooled that old gray fox out at Peck's Swamp that evening. And it fooled the one along the railroad down at Beer Can Alley. Then there was the red fox at the Christmas tree farm out past Jack Hatfield's fur buying place. And let's not forget the gray that the Old Man shot against the snow that full-moon night on the swamp in back of Clonch's house. And then there was…but I'm getting ahead of myself.

For those of you who haven't had the pleasure of sitting bundled against the cold surrounded by nothing by moonlit night while a series of hideous squalls and screams issue forth from a hard-plastic box – well, it's difficult for me to describe what you're missing. You haven't seen the eyes, wandering, darting back and forth. Two glowing embers ignited by the 6-volt lamp on your hat. A shine. A blink. And they're gone, only to reappear 10, maybe 20 feet away. Or closer. And you haven't tried to pry apart the blackness of Midnight using only your eyes as your imagination conjures up a movement here and a four-legged figure there. Is it? Or isn't it? A flicker of motion as the sun rises, and the *snap* of a safety, razor-sharp against a November chill. A wisp of smoke wrapped in tawny fur that comes and goes at will. They're ghosts, these things we call predators. Their game is survival and they can make us, the most intelligent of mammals, look foolish time and time again. And you know what? They're good at it. That's what makes them so interesting, intriguing, frustrating, and addicting.

Over the past 30 years, I've had the privilege of meeting and hunting with dedicated waterfowlers; men and women who spend every waking moment thinking and talking ducks and geese. And then there are the turkey hunters, those sad-sack gluttons for punishment; nonetheless, dedicated and committed, they are. Or should be. Still, I have yet to see any group as fanatical as the predator hunters. Just mention the word *coyote*, and their eyes glaze, and they develop a 1,000-yard stare that looks not beyond you, but through you, to the next hill or the second draw. They are looking to that fresh-snow at midnight some 10 years ago, or 10 years in the future. How would I describe it in one word? Awesome. That's how.

Predator hunting: A glossary

Where do I begin? Do I start with fox? If so, then red fox or gray fox? Maybe coyotes? Crows? Or perhaps I should start with the equipment; however, what type of equipment? Guns? Calls and callers? And what about set up, wind direction, decoys, and scent elimination? *WOW!*

Bipods, such as the ones this team employs, ensure a steady rest regardless of the situation.

Okay, so after the coffee wore off, I came up with this thought. Because not everyone's as well versed in the ways of predators and predator hunting as is Tad Brown or Gary Roberson or Gerald Stewart, I figured that perhaps a glossary of terms might not be a bad idea. A place to start, so to speak. I'll provide something in the way of definitions so that we're all working on the same page. So with that all said, let's spend a few minutes and get to know the predator hunter through his vernacular.

Ammunition – This one's pretty self-explanatory; however, I'll go so far as to say that which you're putting in the chamber of the firearm you're carrying into the field. 'Nough said.

Binoculars – An indispensable item, regardless of your quarry. Often, the predator hunter, a mobile individual, is well served by a lightweight compact binocular. The binoculars should be easily and conveniently carried into the field. A good 10x50 model made by a reputable manufacturer such as Nikon, Bushnell, Bausch & Lamb, and the like will do nicely.

Bipod – One of the greatest inventions since the Ziplock bag has been the fold-away bipod, the one that attaches to the sling swivel stud on your pet centerfire rifle. A flick of the wrist, and the expandable legs drop into position. If you don't already have one, get one. It's that simple. I'm currently using

the Roto-Tilt model from B-Square (800-433-2909), a fine unit; however, Harris also makes a nice outfit, as does a company by the name of Versa-Pod. Single-leg monopods are also available. It really doesn't matter what it's called or who makes it. A steady rest will make you a better marksman.

Black bear – Only recently has black bear calling gained in popularity, although residents of states such as Washington, Colorado, Vermont, and Maine have been doing it for quite a number of years. Your average black bear weighs 200 to 250 pounds, give or take; however, larger specimens, like the 600-pounder recently killed near Washington's Long Beach Peninsula, are out there.

Bobcat – As elusive an animal as there is, second only to the mountain lion. Bobcats are surprisingly well distributed across the United States from Northeast to Southwest, and everywhere in between. In true cat fashion, bobcats tend to come to a call v-e-r-y slowly….sitting and listening, then listening and sitting. They are never in a hurry. Bobcats are taken both by callers and by houndsmen.

Calling – This is simply the art of creating sounds intended to attract and lure into shooting range any number of predators and varmints. Typically, these sounds can be classified one of two ways – food-related, such as the traditional cottontail in distress, and species-related, like the gray fox pup or coyote pup in distress sounds.

A fine winter 'cat, one of hunting's most challenging and elusive species.

Though slowly being pushed into obscurity by CD and digital callers, there are still plenty of good, old-fashioned cassette callers available.

Camouflage – It's no different than turkey hunting, folks. There's only one rule when it comes to predators and most varmints – There is no such thing as an insignificant detail.

Cassette – One of several media on which sounds are recorded. Cassette tapes are still popular; however, they're becoming less so with the advent of compact disk and digital recordings.

Centerfire – The long-range shooter's choice of weaponry. Calibers will differ depending upon the target animal, but can range from one of the .22 caliber centerfires (.220 Swift .222, .223, and the national favorite, the .22-250) through the .30 caliber arms.

Coaxer – (1) A type of call, often consisting of a rubber bulb and an internal reed. When squeezed, air rushing out of the bulb crosses the reed and makes a low-volume, yet high-pitched sound. Meant to imitate a mouse, rat, or other small rodent. This is typically a short-range call. (2) The sound made by such a bulb-type call.

Compact disk – This is another medium onto which sounds are recorded. Gaining in popularity for their ease of use, clarity and authenticity of sound.

CD callers, such as this unit from Lohman, offer some of the highest-quality sound reproduction possible. Multi-speaker packages, too, can prove effective.

Fellow outdoor writer and coyote hunting fanatic - Yes, that's appropriate - L.P. Brezny, with a pair of Nebraska Sandhills dogs.

Cone of sound – The cone-shaped collection of sound waves moving in a defined direction outward from a speaker or other source. What the hell does that mean? Just stand in front of your home stereo speaker. There – you're standing in the cone of sound. Often, predators will maneuver themselves in relation to your location not only to take advantage of the wind – meaning they'll move downwind of the sounds they hear – but they'll also attempt to put themselves into this cone of sound, theoretically in order to hear and pinpoint the source more accurately.

Cottontail in distress – Without question, this is the most popular sound recreated by predator hunters. Cottontail distress cries can be imitated easily using either mouth or electronic calls, and are attractive to a wide variety of predators as well as birds such as crows, hawks, and owls.

Coyote – I think Gary Roberson, owner of Burnham Brothers Game Calls, put it best. "Coyotes are my first

love. The reason is that the coyote is the best athlete on this continent. His reaction time is extremely quick. His speed is good, and his stamina is unbelievable. His senses are extremely keen. I'd compare his sense of smell to that of a bull elk, his eyesight to that of the wild turkey, and his hearing is as good as any bobcat's. You put all that athleticism and keen senses in one body, plus an I.Q. like that of a Labrador retriever – well, that to me is the ultimate animal on the continent." Do I really need to say any more?

Crows – I don't know who said it, but someone once said – "If men were birds, few would be wise enough to be crows." Everyone's seen crows; however, not everyone's hunted them. If you haven't hunted these incredible black birds over decoys with a call, you're missing out on some of the world's finest and most challenging wingshooting.

Decoys – Hunters use two- or three-dimensional representations of, well, things. Typically in the case of

Mouth calls like the one the author plays here are, to many, the epitome of calling convenience. Versatile, no batteries, lightweight, inexpensive. Need more?

predators, decoys come in the form of a food source. A rabbit, fawn, chicken, pheasant, or something of that nature; however, in the case of crows, the decoys may be that of the target animal. Decoys can serve one or more of three purposes – (1) to divert the quarry's attention away from the hunter, (2) to complete the illusion that the calls and calling began, and (3) to bring or maneuver the quarry into shooting range or position.

Drive – An uncommon fox hunting method similar to the popular deer drive. Walkers attempt to push or drive fox to within shooting range of standers. Sometimes it works; most of the time, it doesn't. Why? Because these critters are too smart, that's why.

Gray fox – Yes, gray fox can and do climb trees. They don't climb like gray squirrels, but they'll climb trees nonetheless. Found from the Plains States to the East Coast and along the Pacific, grays prefer more brushy country than does his red counterpart. Like gray squirrels, gray fox are aggressive, often coming to a call like Oprah Winfrey running to the sound of a Big Mac being unwrapped. Often weighing no more than 10 pounds, grays are beautifully colored in their browns and blacks, rusts and whites.

Hounds – Dogs are wonderful field companion, and a tremendous asset to the predator hunter, regardless of

whether he's after coyotes, 'coon, fox, black bears, or cougar. Have you ever heard a redbone barking treed, or seen a Russian wolfhound-grayhound mix run? You won't likely forget either one.

Howler – A mouth-operated call used to reproduce the yips, barks, growls, and howls of a coyote or pack of 'yotes. Typically, howlers are used as a sort of canine locater call – You howl, the coyotes howl back, and you know where they are. In other instances, howlers are actually brought into play as a means of challenging and therefore attracting a coyote or coyotes into shooting range. I find coyote howling a lot like the Primal Scream Therapy that was so popular some years ago. You know, where you paid a doctor lots of money to yell as loud as you could and, the theory was, you'd feel better? Try coyote howling. It's cheaper and just as effective.

Inflection – A fancy word for feeling, or the act of putting feeling into your calling sequences. A good caller can make it sound like you've just closed your hand in the truck door. The more feeling – inflection – you put into your calling, the more natural it will sound. Try to sound hurt. Think about pain and anguish. Pretend your wife just told you – "Honey, Mom's going to come live with us for a while. Clean out that room with all your guns and clothes and fishing stuff, will ya?"

Lanyard – Another fancy term for that necklace that holds all your mouth calls. Actually, a lanyard is an excellent idea. It keeps everything handy and organized.

Long-range – AKA long-range calls. These high-volume noisemakers really reach out and touch things. Some callers prefer to begin their sequence with a long-range call, thinking they will first get the critters in close and then work on them with soft tones. Then there are those who believe that starting with a long-range call can actually frighten away animals that are close. This is known as blowing them out. Long-range calls do come into their own in big, open country like that found out West, and under windy conditions such as are always found in Texas and South Dakota.

Medium-range – These calls are not loud and not soft, and work best in the 100- to 200-yard range, give or take. Again, the key is trial and error.

Mountain lion – A.K.A. cougar, puma, and "Oh-my-God! Did you see the size of that cat??!!" Cougars inhabit much of the West and Southwest; however reports and actual sighting of mountain lions in the Midwest and South are becoming more and more commonplace. Traditionally, cougars have been hunted with hounds, but with states such as Washington now prohibiting the use of dogs –Blame it on Seattle – some enterprising individuals have traded their canines for calls, and with good success. A suggestion for those looking to try calling mountain lions: Take a friend. Take a friend who can shoot well, and doesn't mind watching your back. This is no tabby cat.

Mouth call – This is an air-operated call blown by mouth. The pros? Mouth calls have an incredible range of volume, no batteries to go dead, and inflection like you wouldn't believe. The cons? Some would say the clarity of sound that comes from the new digital or compact disk callers can't be matched by those blowing the traditional mouth calls. I disagree, but the choice is yours.

Patience & persistence – Tad Brown, MAD Calls' chief predator man, claims that these are the two most important characteristics of the successful predator hunter. The only quality I'd add to Brown's list would be self-discipline.

Pelt – This is an animal's furred hide. Often, the term pelt is reserved for when the former owner and the hide have been separated from one another through the skinning process.

Prairie dogs – These squirrel-sized ground-dwelling rodents are creatures of the Plains States and the

The red fox. Old Reynard. Whatever you call 'im, he's as slick as they come.

American West. These varmints provide fine targets of opportunity for long-range centerfire rifle enthusiasts. Prairie dogs live in large colonies called towns, some of which can cover dozens upon dozens of acres.

Predator – These animals prey upon another creatures. Though omnivorous, mammals such as foxes, coyotes, bears, and raccoons are also considered predators.

Prime – The word prime is used to describe a pelt that is as dense and luxurious as it's going to get. In a prime pelt, the underfur is thick and the guard hairs are long, fully-formed, and abundant.

Raccoon – It's said that man has yet to build a container or structure that a raccoon can't get into once it's set it mind to gaining access. With their bandit's mask and heavy ringed tail, the raccoon is a familiar figure from coast to coast. Few activities conjure up visions of tradition and camaraderie as does 'coon hunting with hounds; unfortunately, as North American fur prices continue to fall, and with little hope of an upturn on the horizon, modern houndsmen are becoming fewer and fewer in number. The same is true of trappers. As a result, many areas of the country are seeing huge increases in 'coon populations, and subsequent annual outbreaks of distemper, parvo, and rabies.

My wife, Julie, is a firm believer in shooting sticks like those shown here. Two hundred yards, she says, is no time for off-hand antics.

Red fox – Whereas the gray fox prefers thick, brushy cover, the red is a creature of more open country, which might explain why more folks have seen red fox than have seen grays. While population densities vary from region to region, the red can be found in all of the Lower 48, plus Canada and Alaska; however, the greatest numbers appear to be in the Plains States, particularly in North and South Dakota. It's been my experience that red foxes don't come to a call as aggressively as do gray foxes, but rather are slow and deliberate – almost catlike in their approach.

Red lens – Here's the way it was explained to me. In a physiological 'trade' so that they might see better in the dark, predators relinquished their ability to see that part of the light spectrum that includes red and colors like it. It has to do with the number of rods and cones – light receptors – the animals have in their retinas. We always snapped a red lens over our traditional white light headlamps. The thinking was that while we could see the animal, the animal in turn would not see the light. What these highly-tuned predators DID see was me swivel-necking my head from side to side in an often vain attempt to spotlight them. The lesson here? Movement will kill you – not them – every time.

Scent – Human scent is as detrimental to your success as a .22-250 is to a 125-yard coyote's health. Some say control your human odor with scent elimination potions. Still others will tell you that if you're serious about consistently killing predators, you need to invest in one of these new-fangled scent-killer suits. And then there are those – and I'm one of these guys – who believe that if you work with the wind, and by that I mean set up wisely and with the wind in your face, the other items and gadgets are simply supplemental. You decide; however, the bottom line is – Scent kills (your chances, that is).

Set-up – Here's a comparison to turkey hunting. The best camouflage and calling is no good if you're not going to set up correctly. Did you take into consideration the wind? Have you silhouetted yourself? Do you have some natural concealment, but not so much as to make moving for a shot impossible? Can you see? Or will that coyote, fox, cat, fill-in-the-blank, see you first? Do you have multiple fields of fire? Survival isn't a game to Mister Coyote, so set-up shouldn't be a haphazard decision on your part. You take the variable known as your set-up more seriously, and you will be more successful from a harvest standpoint.

Shooting sticks – Lightweight, often collapsible or folding sticks that when crossed provide a steady rest for the long-distance centerfire shooter. Some models break down into a neat, easily carried foot-long package; others consist of two aged hickory branches, a length of binder twine, and a truckload of sentimental value. Either way, sticks, like bipods, can help make you a better marksman.

Shotgun – The preferred firearm for those predator or varmint hunters who like their action up close and personal. For years and for countless foxes, I carried a 1966 vintage Mossberg Model 500 – with Poly-Choke, no less! – filled with 3-inch hulls containing 2 ounces of copper-plated #BBs. Sometimes, the third 3-inch round would hold 41 pellets of #4 buckshot. Can you say devastating? Today, Julie and I will often tag-team predators, with her carrying a Remington Model 700 in .243 Winchester, and me carrying a Remington Model 11-87 filled with 3-inch #BBs. Thirty yards or 300 – we've got it covered.

Sign – Revealed through a process known as scouting, sign consists of things left behind. These would include droppings and tracks, clumps of fur on barbed wire fences, remains of prey animals, and, ideally, sightings of the animals you are after. All of this information should lead to one inescapable conclusion – Hunt Here.

Gerald Stewart doing what he does best. In the place he likes to do it - Texas.

Few things get a predator hunter's blood pumping like a fresh-fallen snow.

Silhouette – You're wearing the latest and the greatest camouflage known to man, and yet if you sit where your outline aka your silhouette is readily recognizable as human to any and all passing critters, you will not score.

Snow – I love snow. It gives predators the munchies, it keeps fair-weather hunters indoors, and it shows me exactly where I need to be on any given day at any given moment. Whereas many varmints – groundhogs, prairie dogs, 'coon – will descend into hibernation, the true predators – coyotes, fox, and 'cats – can often be seen on the move well into the morning as they seek to fill their bellies with whatever prey hasn't gone underground. That means more productive hunting hours for me. Did I mention I love snow?

Squeaker – See coaxer. Squeaking can be done without the use of a call, simply by kissing the back of your hand and making a high-pitched, well, squeak. I've fooled more than one coyote with this very traditional trick. So has Gordy Krahn.

Starlings – A lot of folks wouldn't put starlings in the varmint category, but I do. Introduced from Europe for its singing voice, starlings can now be found, often in huge numbers, in every state in the Union, where they're not liked by anyone. In the winter, starlings often gather in immense flocks, often near a source of food such as a feedlot, where they can be a hoot to hunt. They are excellent wingshooting practice, and from what the Europeans claim, a pretty good bird on the table. Sorry, but I can't vouch for that.

Texas – Birthplace of Johnny Stewart and son, Gerald, as well as Burnham Brothers' headman, Gary Roberson. Texas is also a hotbed of predator hunting activity, with coyotes, gray fox, and bobcats high on the menu. Want varmints? There's always feral hogs, which also make for some incredible eating.

Tracking – See snow. There's nothing more exciting than getting on a fresh fox or coyote track in a new-fallen snow, and working your way cross-country. Here in Iowa, we'll drive around a complete section (640 acres). Find tracks going in but not going out, and we're in business.

Varmint – In my world, *predators* and *varmints* are two different things. *Predators* include coyotes, fox, and bobcats, or things that eat other critters. *Varmints*, on the other hand, consist of groundhogs, prairie dogs, crows, starlings – things like that. Are varmints, as Webster's dic-

Joe Hassman and his father, Joe Sr., prepare for some long-range action in southwestern Ohio. The target? Groundhogs.

Woodchucks & rockchucks – Woodchucks are also known as groundhogs; *not* groundchucks as my Mother once asked – "Are you going groundchuck hunting, honey?" I hated to have to explain that not only weren't cows in season, but Bob Dutcher would be very displeased if I started throwing .243 Winchester rounds at his prize heifers. Woodchucks live in holes they dig in the ground; rockchucks, on the other hand and as their name would imply, live in the rocks. To further differentiate, groundhogs are primarily at home in the East, while rockchucks are a Western critter. Young groundhogs, by the way, are excellent eating, with a taste very similar to rabbit. Technically these are varmints, not predators, but does it matter?

Yellowhammer woodpecker – Most predators won't hesitate to amend their rodent diet to include birds, and the yellowhammer's screaming distress cry appeals well to this weakness for fowl. Burnham Brothers' Gary Roberson lists the yellowhammer as one of the old standbys. "Without a doubt," Gary said, "the two best-selling sounds out there today are the cottontail duet, and the yellowhammer woodpecker."

tionary defines them, "objectionable?" They can be problematic, like when your prize thoroughbred steps in a groundhog hole and breaks his leg, but objectionable?

Volume control – We've already discussed coaxer/squeaker, medium-range, and long-range, all of which relate directly to volume **and** the distances you need to cover between your position and a potential target. As it does in any type of calling, volume here depends on several variables including weather – particularly wind – and terrain. I will say this. If you can see a coyote and you decide to call, you'd better be damn sure you're next to invisible because he WILL know where that sound came from.

Wind direction – It's been said that if wild turkeys could smell like a whitetail or a black bear, we'd never kill one. I'm prone to believe that one. The same holds true for all predators. Not the varmints so much, but the predators. Critters like coyotes and fox earn their keep and keep their hides attached thanks in large part to an incredible sense of smell. Wind direction and paying attention to it plays a big role in your success, or your failure. Rule number one: Keep the wind in your face. Rule number two: Keep an eye downwind as predators will often attempt to circle downwind of the sounds they're hearing, in part out of suspicion and in part out of a want to pinpoint the source of the sound more accurately. And rule number three: Don't ever forget Rule number one.

So now that we're all on the same page in terms of – well – terms, I'm going to turn this over to one of the most knowledgeable all-round outdoorsmen that I've met – Tad Brown. At 43, Brown has, (pardon the cliché) forgotten more about trapping and predator hunting than most folks will ever learn. And though none of his teachers were ever as famous or as well-known as Tom Miranda or Judd Cooney, Brown nonetheless learned his craft from Old Man after Old Man after Old Man.

But you want to know the neatest thing about Brown? Plain and simple, it's his love of the sport. It's the respect he shows the coyote and the bobcat and the gray fox, not only through his words but through his actions. His enthusiasm is evident whenever the talk turns to one of the greatest things ever to come down the evolutionary pipeline – that incredible creature known as the predator.

Tad Brown on predators

Tad Brown is a member of Mark Drury's MAD Calls team, and the man largely responsible for the conceptualization and creation of many of the team's finest game calling products. This Missourian is a self-proclaimed predator-hunting fool. Mark Drury, himself an award-winning competitive caller and well-versed outdoorsman and predator chaser recently said, "If you want to know anything about hunting predators, especially coyotes, you need to get in touch with Tad. The man's just incredible when it comes to hunting predators."

But how did this bearded gentleman from Preston, Missouri, come to this sport?

"The first successful predator hunt I was on? An old man had an old Burnham Brothers record player –a regular record player. And I went to school with his boy, and one afternoon, he said that he'd take his boy and me out. I remember that the boy was going to operate the player. The old man went to the left and I went to the right. Well, by the time I got over to the log that they told me to and sat down, the boy shot. Within moments, actually. Well, he'd called in a coyote and killed it. I was hooked," said Brown.

"Well, I couldn't afford a record player," he continued. "So I went down to the hardware store and bought the first predator call I could get my hands on. I just kept trying and trying and trying, and then one night in the moonlight, me and a buddy called in a gray fox and I killed it. And like I say, after that, I was hooked."

Tad Brown on foxes

Me: Which is more challenging to bring to a call – red fox, or gray fox? Or is there even a difference?

Tad: A gray fox, to me, responds to anything well. Rabbit distress, bird distress sounds, loud calling, soft calling. He seems to respond well. But I do seem to have better luck with reds. They seem more cautious to me. If I think I'm calling specifically to a red fox, I'll start out with a low, coaxer type call. And often that's all I'll use is that coaxer call. Now, I don't know, but I have called in reds unexpectedly using a regular predator call; still, when I'm specifically focusing on reds, I use that coaxer call and have better luck.

Me: Okay then, Tad, what is it specifically about a gray that makes him respond to a call better?

Tad: I think part of the reason that gray fox respond to a call better is that they're more aggressive and they're not as afraid. I mean, if a red fox is responding to a call and a coyote pops out on the scene, that red is gonna get the hell out of there. But a gray fox? I don't think that's necessarily true. I think a gray fox might take his chances. He's a little more ballsy – even with a coyote. (NOTE – At this point in the interview, I let out a not-so-subtle *hum-mmmm*, an unintelligible groan that Brown immediately translated as my being a non-believer; hence, his next statements). A gray can climb a tree, and he can climb quite well. He'll run in a bush or go underground. You know, a red's really nice and smooth and silky, where a gray is – well, he's a brawler. I'd compare the gray fox to the farm hand and the red fox to the city slicker that works in the downtown office.

Me: Simple question here – Day hunting? Or night hunting?

Tad: Over the years I've had much better success at

Here is MAD Calls' Tad Brown, one of the Midwest's premier predator hunters. Tad's in the hat, by the way.

night. I think that nighttime is the fox's time, especially reds. My experiences with red fox are somewhat limited, just because we don't have many red fox in my part of the country. I'm more about grays and coyotes and bobcats. But I think that the red fox is spookier and feels more comfortable under the cover of darkness. The grays – well, they'll respond at daybreak and in the evening, but I've never had much success with grays during the day.

Tad Brown on coyotes

Me: What's the biggest mistake you see newcomers make when it comes to hunting coyotes?

Tad: It all has to do with confidence, number one – then patience. And probably number three, persistence. I mean, we've got a lot of coyotes in this country, but to be honest with you, we only get a response out of about every 10 stands. A guy may call at eight places or so and not get a response, and he's thinking – "Hell, I've done this a dozen times and I haven't called in anything." But then he goes two or three more times, and one of those times is the magic one. It's just like fishing. The more you catch, the harder you're going to fish and the longer you're going to stay. For the first-timer who doesn't get that immediate success, I know it's difficult for him to stay focused and accurate and confident.

I agree with Brown. And while I personally have killed more reds at night, a wailing rabbit played mid-morning doped this cherry Iowa red fox. When they're hungry, they'll come.

Me: What role does howling play in coyote hunting?

Tad: I use howling to try to locate a coyote. I like to howl before daylight and after dark, and try to get that response. It's like bugling an elk and getting that answer. NOW you know which direction to head. I like to use my howler in another way. You know if you get multiple coyotes to come in and you get lucky and kill one. Or you get real lucky and kill two, and the last one's heading for home and Mother – you can take your howler and do a little coyote distress. A little yipping and yawling, and sometimes that runner will stop and look, giving you one more chance at a standing shot.

Me: How long will you typically stay at a calling location? Or is there any such thing as a "typical" period of time?

Tad: It depends on the situation. If I'm just recreationally hunting, just for myself, and I'm out that first hour in the morning or that last hour after dinner, I may sit for 20 or 30 minutes, and then move on. But if I'm

hunting a contest or for fur, or if I have you out and I'm really busting my butt to put some coyotes in front of you, I'll probably only spend 10 minutes at a spot.

Me: We're reading more and more about the use of decoys among predator hunters. Your take on decoys for things like fox and coyote and 'cats?

Tad: I'm all for decoys for everything. Maybe more for bobcats, but for coyotes and fox, too. And here's something to think about when it comes to decoys, not only for fox but for all predators. You know, I like a little composition, not only when I hide but with my decoy as well. And I'm going to use a neeked lady analogy here. If you're walking through the timber and you look over and there's a gal behind a bush, and she's obviously got her clothes off, chances are you're going to maneuver yourself through the woods there so you can get a better look, if not an eyeful, right? Now if she's standing in the wide open, you got an eyeful. Same with a predator or a turkey or whatever that's responding to a decoy. I like to use a little brush, just enough so that that bobcat or turkey or whatever can see that decoy but can't get an eyeful of 'im. It seems like if that animal can't see the decoy completely, he'll have a tendency to want to get closer. Or at the least position himself where he can see more of that decoy.

Tad Brown on bobcats

Me: Are there more bobcats out there, Tad, than folks think?

Tad: Absolutely! They're very secretive, and while their numbers are fine, their populations aren't like that of foxes or coyotes.

Me: I watched one of your 'cat hunts on the latest Lohman video, Predator Challenge II. And on that one, I watched a bobcat come into a call and sit down. And if you didn't know that 'cat was there, there's no way in hell you would have seen him. Their camouflage is just excellent. So that said, Tad, how in the hell do you see them?

Tad: The first time my Dad took me deer hunting, he told me, "Don't look for something the size of a deer. Look for something the size of a dog or a coyote." So how you spot a bobcat is not to look for a bobcat. Look for something smaller. Keep your eyes peeled for the slightest little movement. Don't expect him to come waltzing in like he owns the place. Lots of times, he's gonna come in on his belly. He's going to slither in, and then he's going to set up. I don't how many times, I'll be sitting there and I'll look up, and there the SOB is watching you. They just appear. How do you spot 'em? Think smaller.

Me: Do you do anything purposely different when you're targeting 'cats as opposed to targeting, say, fox or coyotes?

Tad: Number one, I use a decoy. One of my favorite 'cat decoys is to take a turkey wing feather and tie a string

Tad Brown, right, with partner and call innovator, Mark Drury, share a morning chasing Missouri dogs. And with some success, I might add.

to it. I'll tie this to a low bush or tree branch, and that feather will twist and turn in the wind. When you're hunting 'cats, the feather and that movement gives him something to see and something to move toward. One of the worst problems with 'cats is that often he'll only come so far, and then he'll just sit down. He'll just stay there forever. And with 'cats, I try not to call too much. Try to play on that "curiosity killed the 'cat" kind of thing. So if I'm calling in 'cat country, I'll call for 60 seconds but then I may wait five minutes before I call again.

And finally, Tad Brown on 'coon

Me: You hear about 'coon hunting with hounds, Tad, but you hear or read very little about calling raccoons. Do you ever purposely target 'coon when you're calling?

Tad: Occasionally. And usually when I'm purposely calling 'coon, it's in a damage control kind of situation, when someone's having trouble with them.

Me: 'Coon tactics?

Tad: I've killed several 'coon that responded to a cottontail in distress, but 'coon respond real well to bird sounds. And if I'm purposely calling 'coon, I'll go where the animals are all the time. Just like if I were trapping them. I'd go to the ponds. I'd go to the lake edge. I'd go to the stream bank. And a guy'll be surprised just how many foxes and coyotes and bobcats he'll get to respond right

Brown took this bobcat on a morning hunt in Kansas. Decoys, he says, play a major role in his success with the kitties.

53

It took two to tag-team this fall ringtail at the edge of a cut-over cornfield, a prime location for many different furbearers.

Courtesy of MAD Calls

down there next to the water. BUT – if you really want a sound that works for 'coon, probably the best sound would be a baby 'coon in distress, or what they call 'coon puppies. It's a maternal deal. I've had 'coon respond very aggressively to this, and I've heard more stories from guys where it's legal to hunt 'coon at night with these sounds that 'coon will run right up your pant leg, if you're not careful.

Other Targets

Those are the most popular predators, the ones with whom folks are most familiar. And while I'd dearly love to go into detail on a long list of additional critters – well, there's a couple reasons why I can't. Or more precisely, won't. First, there's the space issue. And secondly, there's the simple fact that this isn't a predator book; fact is, Mike Schoby has handled that subject quite well in his recently released first work, *Successful Predator Hunting*, another project in the *Successful Hunting* series from Krause Publications. What am I trying to say here? Just this – If you're interested in learning predators and predator tactics from A to Z, get a copy of Schoby's book; however, as far as other predators and varmints are concerned, I do have these words.

Black bears – Dear friend and lifelong

Washington resident, Tony Miller, loves to call black bears. And he's damn good at it. For those of you new to the game, Miller has these words of advice – "Get in quiet. You're better off if you've scouted the area prior to the hunt. Call as long and as continuously as you can. And use a scent cover or eliminator." The thing about bears, Miller says, is that while they can't see very well, they have one of the best noses in the wild. "And," he continues, "you'll be amazed at how quietly something that big and heavy can move through the brush. People underestimate bears, and that's a mistake."

Cougars – I've never done it, so I can't say much more about calling cougars than this – Take a friend, and go heavily armed. If, however, your goal is a 'cat rug for the den, my suggestion is to search the Internet or consult a reference such as the current *North American Hunting Club Resource Directory*, and find yourself a guide in Idaho, Montana, Wyoming, or Utah who specializes in hunting lions with hounds. From what I understand, it's an awesome adventure; but – another word of advice if you do that – Be in shape. Hounds and houndmen don't know the meaning of the words, "I'm tired. Can we stop now?"

Crows – My Pop's hunting partner, Ben Scott, is about as fanatical a crow hunter as I've ever seen, short of my aforementioned buddy, Tony Miller. Scott is so crow-crazy that he – get this! – did a self-mount taxidermy job on a road-killed groundhog he found, and uses this fake, along with half a dozen crow decoys, in a macabre sort of "Look what I found! Come and get yourself some of this!" decoy arrangement, often in cut winter wheat or soybean fields. Personally, I've never heard anything like it, but Scott claims it works. And works well. And who am I to question a man so dedicated as to carry a dead woodchuck around with him in the truck?

Starlings – I wouldn't have believed it if I hadn't seen it myself, but starlings, pressured by the gun, can and will get smart – so smart that they'll flare wildly from unnatural movement and the uncamouflaged human form. But if it's fast action you're looking for, find yourself a feedlot or an old barn roosting site in February. Get permission, which usually isn't difficult as few farmers or cattlemen like starlings, then truck a couple cases of low-brass #8s or #9s into the field. Oh, and you can forget about gloves. A hot gun barrel is all the handwarmer you're going to need.

Pigeons – I love hunting pigeons – rock doves, city pigeons…whatever you want to call them. Over the years, I've used a couple methods. You can find a field where the birds are feeding, often after they've taken a short flight out of the nearest metropolitan area, and decoy them. Pigeons decoy extremely well, and while there are com-

Julie's boy, Adrian, and I use monofilament fishing string to hang these crow decoys up high prior to a hunt. Often, the fun part's getting them down.

mercial pigeon blocks available, I've always just used the first three or four casualties in an impromptu spread. The other method involves two hunters and a barn. The shooter stands outside the haymow window, while the driver goes inside and commences to pound on the walls with a stick. You see where I'm going with this?

Groundhogs – Ah, groundhogs. The summer spent in the stubblefields. Or in the second story of Bob Dutcher's barn, which by the way made a tremendous hide for the then rodent-sniper team of my father and me. Groundhogs are the eastern U.S. counterpart of the prairie dog, minus, that is, the controversy. Centerfire, rimfire, archery, muzzleloader, handgun – any and all can and have been used to end the excavating careers of many a whistlepig. And a final note – As I mentioned earlier, young groundhogs are excellent tablefare. Simply substitute the word "groundhog" for "rabbit," and follow your favorite recipe.

Julie's Little Jet with a fine pigeon that happened by during a September dove hunt in Ohio. Jet doesn't care what she retrieves.

4

Bowing To Tradition – Grouse and woodcock

"What a mystical six-letter word – G-R-O-U-S-E."
~ Dwight "Doc E" Erickson

I was born and raised in Iowa, and hardly ever heard the word grouse, nor had I ever seen a grouse until 1979, when my wife, son, dog, and I moved to the beautiful state of Washington. So in the late summer, some 23 years ago at the age of 36, I went hunting for grouse for the first time in my life.

That first season allowed me to shoot a great many boxes of shotgun shells. I bagged four birds. I didn't have the luxury of a grouse hunting mentor or a great book like this one, but in the years that followed, I learned a great deal about the three species of grouse that we have here in the Pacific Northwest. Although my first season as a grouse hunter was pretty dismal, I became immediately addicted. And in the years that followed that first season, I have harvested nearly 500 of those wily birds.

Grouse season is the first bird season that we have here in Washington. Our season has always traditionally begun on September 1st, and continues until the last day of the year. Because of the time of year that season begins, we start hunting in the last days of summer among the beauty of the mountains, the foliage, the aromas, and the ripening wild berries. At night, we are reminded that autumn is just around the corner. By the time that grouse season has been open only a month, the leaves are starting to show their fall colors, and the air has the crispness and smell that hunters all over the world have come to enjoy. Now's the time when the favorite foods of the grouse have ripened, and during the hunt, my dog and I enjoy the flavor of a few thimbleberries or wild raspberries as much as the grouse do.

Grouse have taught me a great many things, especially that they're unpredictable.

Will the bird sit tight for a point from the dog? Will the bird freeze and look like a rock or a piece of wood? Will it remain visible or become completely concealed? I can't count the times that I've snuck up on a grouse that turned out to be a rock. And I can't count the times that I've passed by a chunk of wood that turned out to be a grouse.

Although grouse can be hunted without a dog, a good dog is invaluable. Invaluable because of the hoped-for increased success, but more for the thrill of watching the transformation from confused pup into veteran grouser. Traditional grouse dogs have always been setters. I, on the other hand, have a very non-traditional grouse dog – Casey –a pointing Labrador. Today, after three seasons of hunting, I have come to the realization that Casey already knows more about grouse and their survival tactics than I do.

So what does grouse hunting mean to me? It means being able to go hunting after many months of counting down the days. It means hunting with my canine and human companions. It means the beautiful sights and the wonderful smells – the sound of leaves crunching under my feet. The dog bell that suddenly stops ringing as Casey goes on point. It's the adrenaline rush at the accelerating, twisting flush of a bird whose turning abilities would leave a Formula One race car driver in awe. Oh, and did I mention some of the finest gourmet eating in the world.

Dwight "Doc E" Erickson – a chiropractor, and a man whose playground is the Colville National Forest and the beauty that is northern Washington. I'm envious, Doc.

Here, Maggie and I look over a ruffed grouse taken in the Gifford Pinchot National Forest in southwest Washington - as fine a 4-million-acre grouse covert as has been grown.

His majesty, the King of the Uplands - the ruffed grouse.

Meet the players

Few birds epitomize tradition and style – classic upland gunning, if you will – more completely than does the grouse. But what's perhaps more interesting than the symbolism of the grouse as a family of game birds is the imagery presented by the individual family members. Here, I'm talking about the blue grouse and its representation in – and of – the foothills of the Canadian Rockies. Imagine the sage grouse and the Old West of Wyoming and the prairie chicken and the sharptail, each at home among the now-forgotten wagon ruts and windswept reaches of the Plains. And then there's the ruffed grouse, as synonymous with Michigan's Upper Peninsula and such New England states as Vermont and Maine as anything might ever hope to be.

But who are these symbols, these harbingers of Octobers, past and present? First off, let's take a look at that grouping of birds known as the forest grouse; later, I'll introduce their prairie cousins.

Ruffed grouse – Mention grouse east of the Missouri River, and chances are you're going to be talking about ruffed grouse. Not ruffled grouse, although I've seen more than one a bit flustered after a close encounter of the #7½ kind, but ruffed grouse. Ruffs are a bird of the northern U.S. and Canada. The best populations can be found in the Pacific Northwest – Washington, northern Oregon, and Idaho – as well as Colorado, Montana, and Wyoming,

and the high mountains of northern California. Michigan, Minnesota, and Wisconsin, too, have fine ruffed grouse numbers, as do Pennsylvania, New York, and the bulk of the New England states. Smaller populations of ruffs inhabit the Virginias, and in some years, the rugged hills of southeastern Ohio can provide above average opportunities. A species prone to cyclic population swings – traditionally a 10-year cycle of rise, rise, rise, and then fall, followed by a rebuilding period – ruffed grouse, with their muted autumn colors of browns and tans, blacks and whites, are plain-pretty creatures, precisely marked to blend with their forest environment. Both sexes sport the trademark neck ruff; however, those of the cocks will be much more predominant. Three distinct color phases of ruffed grouse exist, with the most frequently encountered showing a black ruff and tailband. Other phases include a beautiful rusty-red, and a smoky gray color.

Blue grouse – Compared to ruffs, blues are what I'll call a high-altitude gamebird. In Washington, for instance, we typically didn't run into the blues until we'd reached 2,000 feet above sea level. Between roughly 2,000 and 3,000 feet, give or take, we'd quite often find an overlapping of species; that is, both blues and ruffs inhabiting the same cover. Above 3,000 feet, though, the game changed to include almost exclusively blue grouse. Over the years and in talking with upland and forest game biologists and managers in states such as Colorado

My first blue grouse taken, I believe, in 1994. Today, I'm still amazed at how large these wonderful birds are.

A cock sharptail struts his stuff on his spring lek, or strutting grounds.

and Montana, this ruffs-low/blues-high rule of thumb seems to hold true regardless of the location. Blue grouse differ from ruffs in both hue – an overall muted bluish-gray – and physical size – 2 pounds isn't uncommon for an adult; otherwise, I find them quite similar in habit and, despite the variable of altitude, in habitat. Biologists recognize two common subspecies of blue grouse – the dusky, found in the Rockies, and the sooty, a bird of the Pacific Northwest.

Spruce grouse – Also known as Franklin's grouse, the spruce grouse is often tagged with the less-than-flattering moniker of *fool hen* due to the bird's apparent disregard of humans as potential predators. The bird sometimes appears unwilling to run or fly or even hide when threatened. Where they are hunted with some regularity – eastern Washington, Wyoming, Montana, Colorado, northern Idaho, northeast Oregon, Minnesota, Wisconsin, and portions of the New England states – the birds can grow to be a bit more timid, and thus more sporting; still, they're often taken as incidentals by hunters seeking ruffs and blues, and not specifically searching for spruce grouse. The cock spruce grouse is a strikingly handsome bird. A black chest gives way to a black-and-white mottled belly, while the back and rump are a speckled or streaked pattern of bluish-gray and black. A black tail fan tipped in light brown and a brilliant red comb over the eye rounds out the wardrobe. The hen

is drab and extremely well camouflaged, a definite plus for ground-nesters such as the spruce grouse.

The Prairie Grouse

Two subspecies – with large enough populations to be hunted – of prairie chicken exist in the U.S., the lesser prairie chicken, and the greater. My experience in Nebraska has been with the greater prairie chicken, which can be found in North and South Dakota, Kansas, and northern Oklahoma, as well as in some southern stretches of Manitoba. Its counterpart, on the other hand, resides in the lower plains states of northern Texas and portions of New Mexico and southern Oklahoma, too. Sharptail grouse, or just plain sharptails as they're commonly called, inhabit portions of 10 states as well as parts of Alberta, Saskatchewan, Quebec, and Manitoba. Research with both chickens and sharptails has been done in the Loess Hills region of western Iowa and in the Show-Me State of Missouri; however, the jury's still out on whether or not these recent reintroduction efforts have or will result in viable populations of either bird.

The differences between the two chicken subspecies are primarily size and, to a lesser extent, coloration. Greater prairie chickens are surprisingly large, very solid birds, tipping the scales at 2 to 2½ pounds, whereas the lesser prairie chicken will often struggle to reach the 1¾ pound mark. Overall, the greater, or simply *chicken* as the folks in Nebraska are prone to call them, are quite like a hen pheasant in color – a mottled array of light browns, dark browns, buffs, and blacks on the back, with a lighter or softer version of the same on the belly. Lesser prairie chickens, as I've learned and been told, are simply lighter, top and bottom, than are their larger brethren.

Chickens differ visually from their prairie cousin the sharptail in several ways, including –

Chickens – Barred breast feathers that run from chest to lower belly; yellow feet; legs feathered to ankle in front, knee or *hock* in back

Sharptails – Breast feathers show a definite 'V' pattern, no barring to speak of; gray feet; white 'fuzzy' feathers go completely to toes all 'round

Sage grouse – Where they're present, sage grouse, North America's largest grouse, are having a tough time holding their own. Holding their own, that is, against such formidable enemies as urbanization and development, drought, wildfire, and the invasion of any number of natural yet non-native foes such as cheatgrass and pinion juniper, both of which compete for space with the sage grouse's one undeniable need – sagebrush habitat. Today, the largest populations of sage grouse can be found in Montana and Wyoming. Hunting these big western birds is not only traditional, but also strictly regulated by fish and wildlife agencies, and still attracts a fair number of participants. Other states – Washington, Idaho, Oregon, Colorado, Nevada, Utah, and California – have smaller numbers. Among North American wild fowl, the sage grouse is second in size only to the wild turkey. An adult male sage grouse can tip the scales at 8 pounds; the hens, often weigh half of that or slightly more.

Ptarmigan – You want to get an Alaska native going without mentioning the Exxon Valdez? Just pronounce the '*p*' in *ptarmigan*, as in – "You know. After we get this Dall sheep off this mountain, what say we go find us some p-tarmigans?" Sure, it'll make you look a little stupid, but it's great fun nonetheless. Let's just hope your outfitter is unarmed at the time you decide to pull this semantic prank. All joking aside, what some might find interesting is that ptarmigan – silent '*p*' – aren't an Alaska-only game bird. True, about 99.8 percent of the tundra grouse killed in the United States are indeed bagged in The Last Frontier; however, white-tailed ptarmigan, the only species found south of Canada, are found in small pockets in Washington, Montana, Wyoming, and Utah. Only in Colorado will a wingshooter in the Lower 48 find the opportunity to hunt ptarmigan, and that but a brief window of time typically running from mid-September through the first part of October. Three North American

The sharptail, center, shows a distinct V-pattern on the chest, while the prairie chicken's breast feathers (right) are heavily barred.

species of ptarmigan are recognized: the rock, willow and white-tailed ptarmigan. Both the rock and willow ptarmigan are comparable in size to the more familiar ruffed grouse; the white-tailed is a bit smaller, often weighing under a pound. Each bird is a mottled combination of browns and blacks and whites during the spring and summer. All three species turn white in winter.

Guns for grouse

Like many discussions on hunting that begin with – The best gun for blank is blank – the subject of grouse and guns is one which, I believe, has no beginning and will most certainly have no end. There are those for whom ruffed grouse and a fine side-by-side, a 20-gauge or perhaps even a 28, are synonymous. Shot charges and sizes are similarly light for these folks, an ounce of #7½ during the early season, and a switch to #6 shot once the leaves are down.

This Plain's uplander prefers a Winchester Model 21 in 12-gauge, a gun which both looks and shoots the part of a fine bird piece.

Delten Rhoades borrowed my Citori Lightning Feather 20-gauge and Julie's lab, Jet, during this late afternoon grouse hunt in the Nebraska Sandhills.

Ask the man who relishes an evening spent hunkered in a fenceline awaiting the afternoon flight of prairie chickens, however, and he'll likely show you a long-barreled 12-gauge stuffed with high-velocity loads of #5 shot. Maybe #6; still, his comment will be that "you never know *for sure* where those sneaky little things are going to show up." Translation – While the birds aren't difficult to kill, the distances involved in pass-shooting can be lengthy. Better to have the range **and** the pellet count and density, he contends, and not need it, then it is to need it and not have it.

For the purposes of grouse and guns, I'm going to be so bold as to separate the subject into *forest grouse* and *prairie grouse*, the distinction being that one (forest) is typically gunned under close quarters, while the other (prairie) is commonly hunted under conditions where the word 'vast' becomes an understatement. Mind you, I do understand there are exceptions to what I just said. I've been privy to them myself. I've seen ruffs in Ohio and blue grouse in Washington flush at 50 yards. And I've had sharptails and chickens both explode out of the Sandhills practically at my toes; however, I'm going to have to use something as a rule of thumb here.

Forest grouse would appear tailor-made for those of you who enjoy a light double shotgun. Either way, the choice will be a light gun, something that tips the scales at right around 6 pounds, give or take. You'll want something that's more than enjoyable to carry all day. Remember, you're going to spend more time packing this

A traditional grouse gun? Probably not by most standards; however, this Remington 11-87 has accounted for its fair share of ruffs, blues, and prairie grouse.

piece up the ridges and down into the valleys and hollows than you are shooting it.

For years, my pet forest grouse shotgun was a Winchester Model 24 16-gauge double –a 1952 model, and my father's first gun. The Model 24 is light, weighing in at only 6.5 pounds. And the 26-inch barrels point nicely, not to mention quickly. Filled with 1-ounce loads of #7½ lead, the Model 24 fits the bill – dare I say perfectly. Today, the 16-gauge sees quite a bit of time in the uplands; however, that time is now shared with another little beauty, this one a Browning Citori Lightning Feather 20-gauge O/U. Like the Model 24, the Citori weighs next to nothing – 5.7 pounds on our digital turkey scale – and is nothing short of a joy to carry in the field. What's more, the Browning is chambered for both 2¾- and 3-inch shotshells, a factor which in my mind makes it just a bit more versatile than the 16 with its 2¾-inch chambers; still, it all boils down ultimately to a matter of personal preference. The fact is, if it can't be killed with the 16, chances are good that it won't be worried by the 3-inch 20-gauge either.

What's the bottom line, if indeed there is one here? The choice of a shotgun for forest grouse is personal. I've seen all types of guns afield, including 28s and .410s, as well as the old rabbit-ear hammered double 10-gauge – with a 20-inch barrel, nonetheless – that a college acquaintance assured me was the "perfect" gun for southeastern Ohio hill country ruffs. And he may have been right; however, after discovering around lunchtime that

he had hunted all morning with both hammers cocked because, as he claimed, "those grouse are mighty fast," I never made a second trip with him just to find out.

The search for the perfect prairie shotgun is, for those to whom it matters, akin to the search for the Holy Grail. First, does such a thing even exist? And if it does, what will it look like? What will it weigh? And what about barrel length? What to feed it? And will it do a fine job of dressing my birds at the end of the day? Light, as in the 5.7 pounds of the Lightning Feather, is nice; however, is a 20-gauge gun enough for the wide open spaces of the Nebraska Sandhills or the South Dakota grasslands? Some days, yes. Other days, a 105 – that's howitzer, mind you – still leaves you undergunned.

While I won't say I've seen it all, I've seen quite a bit in terms of the arms that folks tote onto the prairies. There've been Benelli Super Black Eagle autoloaders and a Savage .410 single-shot. Citori Model 525s – a wonderful upland gun, by the way, should you have an extra $3,000 lying around gathering dust – Winchester SuperX2 semi-autos, and even a Model 21 side-by-side. Oh, and I've seen plenty of old reliable Remington 870 Wingmasters, 1100s, and fancy "I'd be afraid to hunt with that for fear of scratching something" over/unders. Regardless of the gun and its cost, the effectiveness of that firearm always came down to one thing – the individual standing behind the butt plate. No more, no less. Other than that, 1¼ ounces of either #4, #5, or #6 shot, depending on the time of year,

Julie caught this flush - and kill - on film. These chickens, plus a stray sharptail, were in thin cover feeding on wild rose hips.

hunting methods, and the birds, and a good set of legs are all you need to be a success on the prairie. Oh, and a Multi-Tool for digging the cacti and sand burrs out of yourself and your dog.

Grousing

I believe I could summarize the grouse hunting tactics employed, regardless of the species or the location, in but four simple words – FIND. FLUSH. FIRE. REPEAT; however, I'm not going to do that. What I will do, though, is give you look at the intricacies (?) involved in first finding these wonderful game birds. Once you find them, you have to bring them to bag. And, should these tips fail you, you're always welcome to use the method I'm personally fond of – FIND. FLUSH. FIRE. MISS. REPEAT.

Hunt the food

That's what the old ridge farmer always told me. And it didn't matter if I was in search of cottontails or fox squirrels or, as was often the case in the Ohio hill country, ruffed grouse – the old man's answer, "Hunt the food," was always the same. Elemental? Yes, but it certainly was sound advice.

While it's difficult to make an across-the-board statement using words such as *always* or *never* when it comes to speaking of wild populations, I can with some certain-

ty say this about grouse – All grouse are the same. That is, all grouse are the same in regards to at least two basic needs, food, and water. Now, the ruff's blackberries or wild grapes may be the sharptail's wild rose hips or waste corn may be sage tips for the sage grouse; still, the fact remains, and the old Ohio farmer's words continue to ring true – Hunt the food.

Wild menus change with each passing week. In order to be and remain successful, a hunter has to roll with these culinary punches. Luckily the tapestry that is the grouse's food chain isn't difficult to unravel. Find white or red oaks standing among greenbriar – or better yet, mixed in with, say, 25-year-old slash or selective tree harvest, preferably not on the ridgetop nor at the bottom, but about mid-way, and you're going to be in the ballpark for Buckeye ruffs. That's not to say that blue skies won't have the birds on the sunny tops or that Old Woman Winter's snow and blow won't put them in the woodgrass-and-tangle bottoms – it will – but you do have to start somewhere. Travelling west, I've discovered over the past couple of seasons that where you find wild rose hips scattered across the Nebraska Sandhills, chances are good that you'll run across both chickens and sharptails. And in Washington, it's been high-air huckleberries in September for the blue grouse, while the low-altitude ruffs are at the same moment feasting on blackberries, salmonberries, and the like. The bottom line is as the old man said – Find the food, and find the birds.

Delten Rhoades with Jet, Julie's 5-year-old lab, who performed very well on Sandhills grouse during her introduction to these unique gamebirds.

Chris Kirby of Quaker Boy with a pair of central New York ruffs brought to bag during an October hunt. Snow and grouse just go together.

Most folks, when they think of grouse hunting, think also of dogs. And of these, I think I'd be safe in saying 95 percent think pointing dogs. Pointers and setters – Doc Erickson's pointing lab, Casey, or Phil Bourjaily's English setter, Ike – are to many who pursue grouse with a fervor as integral a part of the hunt as are the birds. Properly trained, close-working dogs such as setters, Brittanies, and Doc's Casey, serve as early warning devices, long-range reconnaissance patrols, and talented retrievers of unknown fallen game, not to mention mute conversationalists, privy to woodland conversations unimagined. Contradictory sort that I am, though, I'm still a fan of our flushing dogs. As are many grousers nationwide. Maggie and Jet, our black labs, have earned their well-deserved stripes on both ruffs and blues in Washington, as well as chickens and sharptails in Nebraska, and on all occasions have performed well. Yes, there have been those times when we've watched a wide-ranging Jet, a black pin-prick against the prairie grass of the Sandhills, race after a rapidly disappearing cluster of similarly-sized points that at one time had been recognizable as sharptails; however, I'm prone to forgive her those transgressions as I sincerely hope she is my occasional severe bouts of inaccuracy.

A word about snow.

I simply *love* grouse hunting in the snow. The woods – or the prairie– are quiet, and dressed in Ma Winter's finest. Then there's the tracking aspect. The period following a new snow is that time when the dogless grouser

comes into his own. Now he can be effective, the birds unknowingly having given themselves and their day-to-day routines away, thanks to the mysteries unveiled by an inch or two of powder. Food – Remember *Hunt the Food*? – becomes even more vital, as internal avian furnaces greedily consume greater and greater amounts of fuel. The pin-oak clusters deserve a look, as do the evergreen blackberries – fruits long gone, but purple-veined green now very much an option. Yes, grouse hunting solo in the snow is the way I learned the sport, some 30 years ago in the slash and hardwood thickets of northeastern Ohio. Looking back, it was a most wonderful education.

Meet the woodcock

Bogsucker. Now there's a hell of a name for one of America's most traditional upland game birds. That's but one of several handles given the American woodcock. Other names include the familiar timberdoodle and the less flattering, mudsnipe.

Woodcock are a bird of the East, ranging from what I'll call the Central Midwest – Iowa, Minnesota, and northern Missouri – to the East Coast, and from Ontario and New Brunswick south to wintering grounds in Florida, Alabama, Mississippi, and Louisiana. In the Upper Midwest, the states of Michigan, Minnesota, and Wisconsin annually post impressive numbers of both woodcock and those who seek them. The New England States of Vermont and Maine, too,

Meet the woodcock, a.k.a. the timberdoodle. His beak's funny-looking, his brain's upside-down, and he's too big for his stubby little legs - but we love 'im anyway.

The length of the woodcock's bill can provide information as to the bird's gender - 2.5 inches or less, it's a male; 2.75 inches or more, a female.

are noted havens and hallowed haunts of the timberdoodle.

Visually, I'll compare the woodcock to a hen bob-white, with its very soft collection of subdued brown, black, gray, and buff, and a bit of white pin-striping scattered here and there. Motionless against fall's leaves, the 'doodle is damn near invisible. This is one reason why dogs play such an important part in the woodcock hunter's arsenal. Woodcock are chunky, short-legged little things. A shorebird, it's theorized, relocated at the whim of evolution off the beaches and moved inland, where today, it scurries under alder and poplar and cedar canopies, safe from avian eyes and sneaker waves.

Of particular interest to most, hunter and non-hunter alike, is the woodcock's bill. Often measuring more than a quarter of the bird's entire length, the 'doodle's bill is used much in the same way as are forceps. The bill is thrust into the soft earth, and the surprisingly flexible tip twisted slightly back and forth as the bird searches for it's favorite meal, earthworms. The bill, interestingly enough, serves a function for the successful hunter. Biologists have determined that male woodcock will seldom sport a bill more than 2.5 inches long; females, typically 2.75 inches of bill. An easy and reliable field test involves using a dollar bill as a measuring tool. If the bird's bill is longer than the bill is wide, chances are almost 100 percent your 'doodle is a female. Females are also physically larger, weighing 7 to 8 ounces, as compared to the male's 5 to 6.

Oh, and lest I forget. Their brains are upside-down – an evolutionary alteration, no doubt – and the males are

Typical woodcock cover in eastern Iowa. Damp and sun-dappled, with little ground clutter, just perfect for the little birds.

prone to singing. In the northern parts of their range each come spring – April, perhaps – the male woodcock performs a mating ritual intended to attract female companions. As daylight fades, the male, from a stage such as a short-grass meadow, launches himself high into the twilight sky. With primary feathers *twittering* softly, he rises almost out of sight; then, suddenly, he begins a wide, spiraling descent, all the while issuing a babbling trill that once heard can never be forgotten. On the ground again, he struts while snorting a nasal p-e-e-n-t! A moment later the sky-show begins anew. I've been privy to the male woodcock's singing routine, and it's fascinating to say the least. One interesting side note should you discover a bird's singing ground – With the male airborne, slowly walk as closely as you can to the spot where the sky-dance originated. Most birds will land very near to where the flight commenced, and if you keep still and low, you'll likely be afforded a close-up look at the mysterious timberdoodle.

'Doodle myths and methods

Myth 1 – Female woodcock will relocate hatchlings by air, carrying them between her legs, should she feel the nest site is threatened. Sorry, doesn't happen. I'm not exactly sure where this one started, but I've been told that such a maternal feat isn't aerodynamically possible. And, just as soon as the little ones are pipped and dry, they're wandering around behind Mama, feeding on spiders and mos-

quitoes and other 'doodle delicacies.

There are two elements to successful woodcock hunting – when, and where. Unlike, say, a rooster pheasant that can be found here and there throughout the whole of a two-month season, woodcock are a bit different. From what I've seen, all woodcock coverts are the same; that is, there's something about each that connects the first to the second, the second to the third, and so on. It's almost as if there was a template, so to speak, and that once you've found 'doodles in Cover A, there stands to reason that there would be birds in Cover B – IF, that is, Cover B is similar. Always? Certainly not, but I've found this impromptu equation to hold true on many more than a single occasion.

What does this woodcock template look like? My experience has shown this to be damp, moist, but not necessarily sopping-wet ground – something suitable for a bird that feeds by drilling into the earth with its bill. This cover is typically sun-dappled, thanks to overhead cover consisting of aspens, poplars, young cottonwoods, and the like. Sometimes this canopy will be cedars; or as I've found in northeast Ohio, young pin-oaks. Ground cover, or more precisely, clutter, in these coverts will be, on a scale of one to 10, a four. Maybe even a three. My theory, and that of others I've talked to, is that the short-legged little birds don't enjoy wading through jungles of thick, tangled, low-lying scrub. Or perhaps they feel a bit more comfortable where they can rely on both their eyes and their incredible plumage to alert them to and hide them

Woodcock droppings, also called 'splashings' or 'chalkings,' are a sure sign that birds are - or were - in the vicinity.

from predators.

Where have I found 'doodles? What has it looked like? In Ohio, for instance, I regularly found woodcock in a buffer strip of poplars and willows that separated Bob Wolfe's cattail duck swamp from the adjoining pasture. Over the years, my father and I saw – and bagged – many timberdoodles over the marsh either right at shooting light or at the close of the day. Across State Route 5 from the marsh, the covert described in the opening paragraphs of this section provided the stage for annual shoots. Both locations shared many of the aforementioned characteristics – relatively young overhead cover, damp soil, and minimal ground clutter. Here in Iowa, my woodcock experience has been much the same. A nearby marsh holds a handful of birds in mid-October, these typically found within a buffer strip between the water and the crop ground. The difference here? Pin-oaks, not willows, cottonwoods, and aspens. And in the northeast corner of Iowa, I shared a morning with hunting partner, Phil Bourjaily, in a covert reminiscent of my Ohio parcel. It had a wonderful creek coursing below a gentle hillside covered with young elm and ash. As far as woodcock templates go, it was perfect; in terms of an experience, it was unmatched.

Myth 2 – The soft, almost musical twittering sound that accompanies the woodcock's flush is made vocally. Again, not true. At first it was thought that this pleasant sound was

indeed coming from the bird's throat; however, an enterprising researcher removed the three outer primary feathers from a most-accommodating test subject, and – surprise! – was left with silence.

Where to go is but half of the equation, because *when* is just as important. Here, we'll introduce another aspect of woodcock hunting – locals, and migrants. Locals, also known as natives, are just that; 'doodles that were born and raised in the vicinity. Migrants, or flight birds as they're sometimes called, are the transients. The birds that appear almost magically in northeast Iowa come mid-October, or those that arrive in Lake Charles, Louisiana, around New Year's Day – give or take a week, of course.

One way to view this southward migration is to take a look at the season dates for several states along a major woodcock thoroughfare such as the Mississippi River Valley. In 2002, opening day in Wisconsin and Michigan arrived on September 21. South, in Iowa, it was October 5, while in Missouri, the opener came on October 15. Continuing south, Arkansas listed November 9 as opening day, and Mississippi and Louisiana both showed the woodcock season beginning on December18 and lasting until January 31. Is this a scientific model? No, but it is meant to demonstrate the timing associated with these migratory wanderers.

Typically, the woodcock opener and local bird populations go hand-in-hand; it's not until later in the season that most hunters will encounter flight birds. Again, using

Iowa as an example, our populations will traditionally peak around October 20. So, too, will the numbers in central Wisconsin, so says a friend who lives and hunts in this game-rich part of the Midwest. However, and going back to Iowa, I have over the past four years noticed greater numbers of birds in the southern part of the state well after the last-Saturday-in-October pheasant opener, and often into the first week of November. As with waterfowl, weather – wind, particularly – plays a role in dictating the timberdoodle's nomadic and nocturnal ways. And until biologists narrow the gap between migratory science and conjecture – well, we'll just have to go with tradition, mystery, and a good-feeling guess.

And finally, there's the *how* factor. There's not much complicated about woodcock hunting. Hitting them – yes – but hunting them…well, I won't say it's easy, but I will say it's relaxing.

Guns & loads – This one's simple. Something light because you're going to carry it a lot more than you're going to shoot it. And something that swings well, particularly in tight spaces. Other than those 'doodles I killed as an early-morning incidental to a duck hunt, my woodcock have all been bagged with either a 6.4-pound 16-gauge side-by-side shooting an ounce of lead #8 shot, or a 5.7-pound 20-gauge over/under filled with ¾-ounce of steel #7. Both models fit the light and quick criteria well, and both, by the way, sport 26-inch barrels, as I need all the help I can get in the quickness department.

With & without – Only twice have I hunted woodcock over a pointing dog, and let me say that both times were wonderful. A good pointer, trained to hunt close, is a tremendous asset to the woodcock hunter, both before the shot and – perhaps most importantly – afterwards, for finding down birds can prove an impossible task even for the sharpest-eyed hunter. A gentleman told us in Nebraska – "It's what a dog does after the shot, M.D., that proves his worth." With woodcock, I believe that whole-heartedly.

Now that I've praised pointers, let me also say that flushing dogs – and our black labs come quickly to mind – can also make good 'doodle dogs. The keys are slow and close. That, and despite the fact that some dogs, for oft-debated reasons, simply abhor the thought of picking up a woodcock, they should at least help find downed birds

And finally, there's the dogless man, a category into which I have most often fallen. The lonely woodcock hunter can be successful; that is, if he moves through the covert slowly and stops often – 'doodles, like roosters, get nervous when the footfalls cease – and commits himself to a thorough search, and then some, after each shot.

I enjoyed carrying this Citori 20-gauge for 'doodles in the fall of '02. Light and short (26-inch), the Lightning Feather was a blessing on those all-day hunts.

Phil Bourjaily, here with his English setter, Ike, and an eastern Iowa timberdoodle.

In many states, dove season provides hunters with the first opportunity to get back into the field…and see how rusty they've become during their seven-month hiatus.

5

Quicksilver – Doves

"You know, Michael D, I could get to like this" ~ Mick Johnson, dove hunting convert

September in the north…cooling temperatures, changing leaves, immense anticipation. It's dove season, and I love it! It is the first time a wing shooter can practice shots and reactions that no sporting clay course can teach. There is no other game bird that can humble even the finest shooters like the dove can. I am certainly no exception to this as I have made many "screw marks" in the ground where a fast flying dove has spun me around in circles. Nonetheless, shooting is fun; and dove hunting gives the greatest opportunity to go through a box of shells.

It, too, marks the beginning of true in-the-field training of your trusty retriever. No matter how many dummies have been thrown nor times the cap gun was fired, nothing compares to the real deal. The excitement in my yellow lab's eyes when I put on my camo and reach for the gun could possibly be my biggest reason for sitting in a dove field. Dove season allows him to recall all the training from the summer sessions. Well, maybe not all; but it is a start!

Of course, the reason so many of us enjoy dove hunting is the social aspect. Gathering friends and family to line a dove field is about as fun as it gets. It is also a great time to introduce youths to the shooting sports.

All these factors make for a great experience in the outdoors for me, and I would bet for most of us. I just look forward to grabbing some friends, the dogs, stools and a box of shells…OK, two boxes.

Rob Paradise – National Sales and Marketing Manager for Flambeau Outdoors, and one of the most enthusiastic dove shooters we've ever seen…even when he's not feeling well. Huh, Rob?

Ah, fruit pies. The essence of dove hunting. Here, Rob Paradise, right, takes a break from his ordinarily refined and dignified demeanor to lunch with the commoners. Or something like that.

Doves Or No Doves?

I feel sorry for those folks in places like Iowa. And Minnesota. There's a three-word reason for my sympathy – no dove hunting.

You see, dove hunting is without question one of the greatest sporting events ever conceived. And I'm here to tell you why.

1. You don't have to wear camouflage to dove hunt. Oh, you can, and most folks do; but, I've killed more than my share of the quick-winged little things while seated on a red-and-white Coleman cooler clad in blue jeans and a gray USMC t-shirt. Yellow buckets also work well as stools, and don't even flare birds. Doves, I've discovered, help you remember that hunting is not a fashion show and the winter wheat field not a runway for camouflaged clothes horses.

2. You don't have to be quiet or still when you're dove hunting. Dove hunting is all about the camaraderie. The joking back and forth. The story telling. It's blatantly drinking a cup of coffee out of a green-and-white Go-Cup while eating a frosted blueberry pie…and not worrying about being completely, 100 percent hidden. It's talking out loud, and not getting yelled at by your hunting partners.

3. You get to shoot a lot when you're dove hunting. And I mean a lot. With spring gobblers, it's one shot. Deer? Same single-shot deal. Or at least it's supposed to work that way. In the case of waterfowl, there's a little bit more in the way of ammunition expenditure; still, it's nothing like doves. Dove hunts have a way of taking everyone back to Stage One in the theoretical Five Stages of the Hunter. You know, the one in which the quality of the hunting experience is measured in terms of the number of times you get to shoot the gun. With me and doves, every hunt is a phenomenal success.

4. There are no $150 calls. And no calling. Yes, Virginia, there are dove calls; however, the only ones I've heard in the field consisted of someone cupping their hands and blowing on their knuckles while fluttering their fingers. You know, that hollow sound we used to make as kids. To the best of my knowledge, it's never actually convinced a dove to alter its course; still, it's extremely easy, and ranks on the Fun Meter right up there with whistling across a blade of grass pinched between your thumbs.

5. Dove guns are light, and usually don't require wheels like some of today's huge specialty shotguns. Oh, yeah, and dove guns are very pretty to look at, particularly those which have been paid for in full. And the recoil from most dove loads doesn't relocate your shoulder to the middle of your back. Dove shells are inexpensive – they have to be! That means you don't hear the cash register *cha-ching!* each and every time you pull the trigger like you do with those fancy non-

Light, pretty, quick, and inexpensive to shoot - the dove gun.

The mourning dove is well known to hunter and non-hunter alike.

toxic rounds that cost $2.25 each.

6. Dove hunting doesn't require much walking, which means that young and old alike can sit on their buckets and be neither tired nor in need of a healthy dose of Aleve the morning after. Put a 6-year-old in the shade with a bottle of Gatorade and a twin-pack of Pop-Tarts, and you have all the makings of a good time. You say your Pop's going to be 70 next spring? Open a lawn chair along the edge of a sunflower field out of the sun, crack a box of shells and a cold drink, and set the Old Man to shooting. It doesn't matter if he hits anything – his smile is more than worth the effort.

7. And finally, doves are quick to clean and damn near without equal on the grill. Just slap half a jalapeno on the bone side of a salt-and-peppered breast, wrap it in bacon, and toss it on the old bar-be-cue cooker. When the bacon's crisp, the dove's done. Like Chris Paradise – you'll meet him later – states matter-of-factly, "Dove breasts and a cold beer. Awesome." That about says it all.

8. All right, one more then. It's just flat fun. Thanks to doves, we're reminded each September that hunting is supposed to be enjoyable. No pressure. No glory. No Boone & Crocket, Pope & Young, or 12-inch beard. There's no annual banquet. No emcee. Only good friends, good eats, and the very best of times…as it should be. Remember?

Meet the players

A walk – a very **brief** walk, mind you – on the Internet revealed there to be more than 300 species of doves and pigeons inhabiting the globe. An interesting detail, to be sure; however, hunters in the United States have but a small handful of these with which to become acquainted.

Mourning dove – This is our most numerous dove, and the one, if you already consider yourself a dove hunter, that you're most likely familiar with. Today, it's hard to find a state without a good to excellent population of mourning doves; however, there are those, and Texas comes to mind almost immediately, that have simply ridiculous numbers of birds. For the most part, the highest densities of mourning doves are going to be found from the Mississippi River west to the Pacific, although states such as Illinois, Ohio, Indiana, Georgia, and the Carolinas certainly do have their share.

White-winged dove – A bit larger than the mourning dove, the white-winged dove traditionally made his home in Texas. In recent years, white-wing populations have moved north-by-northeast to where today, numbers of these fast-flying birds can be found in Oklahoma, Nebraska, Kansas, and even up into parts of Missouri. Friends around Austin, Texas tell me that

It's the social aspect of dove hunting, many claim, that pulls countless hundreds into the fold, and I couldn't agree more.

Texas has traditionally been home to the majority of the country's white-winged dove population; however, the birds are becoming increasingly numerous in Oklahoma, Nebraska, Kansas, and parts of southern Missouri.

because white-wings are a bit more aggressive than are the mourning doves, populations of the larger birds are ousting mourning doves from much of their original range.

White-tipped dove – This is another Texan; actually, a south Texan. According to literature from the Texas Parks & Wildlife Department, the white-tipped dove is similar in appearance to the white-winged variety, with the major differences being a slightly larger overall size and a rusty-red coloration to the underwings.

Inca and ground doves – I mention this pair of non-game and protected species simply because they're doves. Both are small, about half the size of an adult mourning dove, with a bit more distinctive markings than either the mourning dove or the white-winged. Distribution? Surprise – Texas.

Eurasian collared dove – I ran across this one while rummaging through the Internet. Originally from Africa, this prolific little beast quickly spread throughout Europe before being blown across the Atlantic – or so scientists believe – onto sunny south Florida during the 1980s. From here, the collared dove marched progressively northward. Today, some pockets can be found as far north as southern Missouri where it mingles with native populations of mourning doves.

When, where, and a brief update

In those wonderful states that do offer hunters the opportunity, dove seasons are traditionally a September thing. Some places, Washington state for instance, begin and end their brief, 15-day season during the ninth month. Others, like Ohio, opt instead for a split season, which typically runs from September 1 through the third week of October. It then reopens during the final week of November. From what I've seen, this is a good thing as hunters are provided both the chance to participate in the warm-weather, early season that is September dove hunting, and aren't forced to sit and watch as those fall or pre-winter flights pass through unmolested. While gunning late November doves in northeastern Ohio may be some of the coldest hunting you'll ever do, when it's hot, I'm telling you it's red hot!

But let's get back to September. While I'm not going to go so far as to say something so maudlin as "September and doves go together like $6 hotdogs and baseball," the fact of the matter is, it's true. Doves, at least mourning doves, like blue-wing teal and pintails, aren't fans of cold weather. It often takes little more than a couple back-to-back chilly evenings, and the whole population heads for warmer climates. Oh, there will always be a handful of hardy stragglers, but for the most part, cold nights means it's time to stop thinking doves and start thinking something else.

When talk turns to the *where* of dove hunting – well, that's another good story. Today, only 11 states don't have a dove season, one of which – I'm ashamed to say – is my current home state of Iowa. It's a long story, but we'll blame Governor Tom Vilsak for that one. The other separatists include Minnesota – By no fault of Jesse's! –, Michigan, New York, Vermont, New Hampshire, Maine, Massachusetts, Rhode Island, Connecticut, and New Jersey. Wisconsin hunters appear to have jumped through the last legal hoop and by the time this project goes to press, the Dairy State could be pulling the trigger on mourning doves.

Annually, the U.S. Fish & Wildlife Service estimates that an astonishing 400 million – that's 400,000,000! – mourning doves inhabit the country, and of these, hunters in those oh-so-lucky states harvest more than 25 million. To squeeze it down even more, I'll venture to say that of these 25 million birds, the bulk are brought to ground south of the Mason-Dixon Line in Virginia, Georgia, and the Carolinas. Mississippi, Louisiana, Arkansas, and Alabama are all states with a strong tradition of dove hunting. In Georgia, for instance, the opening day of dove season ranks right up there with Christmas and the first day of the state fair, combined. The same is true in Kentucky. And then there's Texas and California, states where the

Chris Paradise, head of sales and marketing at O.F. Mossberg and committed .410 dove shooter, and my Pop, Mick, share a laugh during an early September hunt in Ohio.

mourning dove annually holds the number one spot as the most popular game animal. Other top dove states include Nebraska, Kansas, South Dakota, and Illinois; still, I find it difficult to single out all but those spectacular southern spots, for as I mentioned earlier, it's hard to find a place here in the U.S. where there aren't doves.

Dove guns and dove gear

"Hey, M.D. What's that kid shooting?"

The disembodied voice coming from the corn was that of my father, Mick. The *kid* he was referring to was one-half of our host team for the morning, Chris Paradise. It was September 2002. Paradise, along with his younger brother, Rob, worked with the folks at the Ohio-based Flambeau Products Corporation, a company known best for its fine line of waterfowl decoys. The firm makes everything from teal to tackle boxes and – let's not forget – Duncan Yo-yos. Avid dove hunters, the Paradise brothers had invited me, my wife, and my Pop out to a parcel of ground near the crossroads town of Mantua so that we might shoot some doves and photography, and – laugh and eat fruit pies while sitting atop yellow buckets at the edge of a standing cornfield.

What my Pop was questioning was the elder brother's choice of weaponry for the morning's shoot. "All I'm hear-

Julie, here with Maggie and Jet, prefers the soft recoil of her custom-fit Remington 11-87 autoloader and Winchester low-recoil rounds.

In a single barrel, I'm a believer in modified chokes. With stacked barrels like on this little 20-gauge Citori, however, I do enjoy the convenience of a full overtop a modified tube.

ing is a little *pop…pop*," he told me once I walked over and knelt next to his folding stool. "Just a *pop*, and then a dove falls out of the sky. What the hell is he shooting?" Fortunately, I'd just recently talked to Chris about his shotgun of choice and had an answer for my father. "It's a .410, Pop," I told him. "A Browning Citori, over-under. He's shooting bismuth #6 shot out of it."

"A .410! Well, I'll be damned," said my Pop, failing in whatever attempt he might have been making to disguise his amazement. And with that, he turned away shaking his head. "A .410," I heard him mutter as I walked back to my own seat. Let me tell you, it was classic.

Bear with me here when I say that doves are a little like squirrels. But before you open your mouth to argue, let me finish. Doves are a little like squirrels in that over the years, they've been fired upon with just about every multi-projectile shoulder-fired weapon known to man. And some single projectile firearms as well, but I'd best keep Daisy BB guns and 12-year-olds out of this.

I've witnessed frustrated waterfowlers blaze away at passing mourning doves with 3.5-inch autoloaders filled with dollar-each loads of steel BBs – a spur of the moment kind of thing, I believe – and I've had the pleasure of watching Chris Paradise bag dove after dove after dove with what my father so kindly referred to as that "little .410." Is there a bottom line here? A perfect dove gun? To my way of thinking, there's probably no such thing as the *perfect* dove gun. Oh, there will be some that might be bet-

ter suited than others for one reason or another, several of which we'll explore here in just a bit; however, the perfect dove gun, I'm going to guess, is all in the eye of the individual behind the butt plate. If you were to gather together 100 dove hunters, chances are good that you'd be presented with at least 80 different makes and models of shotguns, not to mention all of the common gauges currently making the rounds in North America.

But, and at the risk of being quite the hypocrite here, I can present my ideas about the perfect dove gun.

Gauge – Although you'll certainly find the 16-gauge, 28, and .410 on dove fields across the country, chances are good that this mythical perfect dove gun is going to come in either a 12-gauge or a 20-gauge format. Why? Well, there are practically an infinite number of variations, meaning makes, models, and options, where the 12 and 20-gauges are concerned. Likewise, prices for these particular gauges will likely fit any wallet, and ammunition is relatively inexpensive – yes, even some non-toxics – and shotshells can be found in just about any out-of-the-way corner grocery in the nation.

Action – Okay, so here's where we get a little muddled; still, I'm going to say that our *perfect* dove gun will be an autoloader. One reason – sustained fire. Doves and the expenditure of ammunition typically go together. So, too, does this expenditure and one of Newton's Laws

Yes, I do wear camouflage when I dove hunt, despite having said that it's not absolutely necessary. I don't want to be the only one in street clothes, eh?

A dove chair doesn't have to be a chair at all. Here, Rob Paradise puts a camo-painted 5-gallon bucket with a cushion swivel lid to use, proving that anything capable of holding LOTS of shells will work.

of Physics that translates into recoil. All this means little more than – If I'm going to shoot 75 rounds during an evening dove hunt, I'm going to greatly appreciate the softer recoil afforded by a gas-operated autoloader. So will the young person or the lady on the stool next to me. But don't toss that over/under, side-by-side, or pump away just yet. Remember, it's all in what you shoot well, regardless of the variables.

Barrel length – This is an element that to me doesn't make much difference. In the past, I've hunted doves with 20-gauges sporting 26-inch barrels, and 12s with 28-inch tubes. Again, and while I hate to keep referring this, the best gun is the one you shoot well. But in terms of the quest for the perfect gun, I'll choose the lighter 26-inch barrel just because I really don't need those two additional inches of steel **and** the additional weight.

Chokes – In a single barrel, I'm a modified kind of guy all the way. Modified – 55 to 65 percent of a pattern inside a 30-inch circle at 40 yards – just seems to be that ideal middle of the road constriction. Combine that with some of today's modern ammunition, particularly the new non-toxics, and we modified shooters are good from 20 yards to 40 yards, and perhaps a little farther. What about double barrels with interchangeable choke tubes? Well, it depends. If I don't expect the shots to be long – say, a hunt over a waterhole, at the edge of a roosting area, or over a

small field – then I'll go with improved-and-modified; however, if the opportunities for longer (40+ yards) exist, then I switch to a modified-and-full combination

Weight and fit – I threw these two in as a "just because." Personally, I like a lighter dove gun, not because I'm going to be carrying it much, but just because I seem to shoot a lighter gun better. As for fit, that's a no-brainer. Like Phil Bourjaily, shotgunning editor for *Field & Stream*, says – "If it doesn't fit you, it doesn't shoot where you look." And it's pretty important to shoot where you look. And vice versa.

Shotshell choice – 1⅛-ounce of #7½ shot in lead, or an ounce in #7 steel. That's in the 12-gauge. For the 20, there's either ⅞-ounce of lead #7½, or ¾-ounce of steel #7. Me? For the perfect fodder for the perfect dove gun, I'll pick the steel – yes, even if the location and the regulations don't require I choose a non-toxic load. Steel's quick, patterns well in these small shot sizes, and kills light-feathered things like doves as well as any lead load. Plus, it provides an apples-to-apples warm-up for waterfowl season. Yes, I'll go with ¾-ounce of steel #7 shot.

Shotgun accessories – Here, I'm referring to items such as slings, camouflage, optics, tube extensions, ported species-specific chokes…you know, things like that. One word – none.

The labs - Jet, with the red collar, and Maggie - are 50 percent of my reason for dove hunting. I wouldn't have it any other way.

other than a gun and a bag full of shotshells in order to be successful. Certainly the ability to repeatedly shrug off misses and shoot half-way decently in the face of over-whelming ridicule from your peers does help; however, what I'm talking about here is gear.

And while dove hunting doesn't require boats and trailers, four-wheelers and 437 calls, deer carts and binoculars capable of seeing mouse tracks on the Moon, there are a few things that can make any dove hunt not only more productive from a harvest standpoint, but just flat more enjoyable. Just a few things, mind you, such as –

Camouflage – Do you need it? Probably not, especially if you can conceal yourself in, on, or behind some sort of natural cover such as standing corn, sunflowers, tall weeds, or – my favorite – a telephone pole. Do I wear it? Yes, but only because I don't want the other folks, my wife included, calling me a nerd. Seriously, though, camouflage has its place in the dove fields. Doves aren't blind, and if hunted to any extent, can grow a little alarmed at seeing a 6'3" clump clad in a Sturgis 2002 t-shirt. In most cases, when we're talking dove camo, we're talking lightweight short-sleeved shirts and pants….maybe even shorts; however, I have hunted in September when an insulated jacket wasn't out of the question. Dress for the weather, sit still, and you shouldn't have any problem.

Dove chair – Some folks use folding chairs specifically designed for dove hunting. Others use small hard plastic totes, which with their padded seats provide not only a place to sit, but storage for what little stuff you take into the field. Me? I use an olive-drab five-gallon bucket – with handle and lid – and an old camouflaged seat cushion, so old that the pattern, I believe, is Realtree's All-Purpose…Heaven forbid! The bottom line here is that it's your chair; therefore, it's your decision on how elaborate. Basically all I'm looking for is (1) a place to sit, and (2) a place for my stuff. My $1 bucket does that relatively well. Typically, my bucket contains –

- bug repellent with DEET….I hate ticks!
- Toilet paper – self-explanatory
- A small first aid kit with bandages, Q-Tips, tape, Bactine
- A canteen of water and a selection of food stuffs, including Oatmeal Pies
- A collapsible water bowl for Maggie, the lab, who won't drink from a bottle
- Ammunition….yes, sometimes I carry *two* buckets!

Cooler with ice – September across most of the country comes complete with heat and humidity, and because of this, there will be times when I'll pack a small cooler into the field. This is particularly true for those hunts where I can drive right up to the stand and

The PERFECT dove gun – Okay, so what do we have here? Sure, I expect some discussion and some old-fashioned argument; however, here's my call – Remington's Model 11-87 Premier autoloader in a 20-gauge. At 6.75 pounds, it's light, and the 26-inch barrel swings well. Because of its gas operation, the Premier's recoil is more than manageable, even on those hoped-for high-volume hunts. The interchangeable choke system allows for some adjustments, depending on the birds and the conditions. So, too, does the 3-inch chamber; however, you're not going to need that in the dove field. As for fit, the length of pull (LOP) of this particular piece is that universal person 14.5 inches; still, a competent stock doctor can change that if it's deemed necessary. Price? Right around $750 – a little more than some pumps, but a lot less than some of the fancier over/unders; but, we can justify the cost – Do we need to do that? – with the fact that the 3-inch-capable Premier can serve double-duty as an excellent upland field gun or, for the more adventurous and those willing to spring for a couple boxes of Remington's new 3-inch 20-gauge Hevi-Shot, a great over-the-decoys duck gun. So there you have it. The dove hunter's equivalent of the unicorn – the *perfect* dove gun. Is this my final answer? No way. But I'd like to think it's a good answer.

As I mentioned back in the beginning stages of this chapter, one of the greatest things about dove hunting is its elemental nature; that is, you really don't need much

If you're going to hunt doves in September with a dog, remember one very simple rule - WATER. Oh, and lots of it.

unload. In the cooler are a couple frozen half-gallon water containers and often a dozen or more 16-ounce plastic bottles of water. When it's hot, there is no such thing as having too much water. Trust me. TIP – A layer of old newspaper and a folded bath towel overtop the ice and water helps keep everything nice and cold. TIP II – A small bolt of camouflage netting or burlap thrown over the cooler turns it into a fine dove chair.

Dog – Dove hunting's no different than most hunting activities. Do you need a dog? No. Do dogs help make the hunt that much better by providing entertainment and companionship, not to mention serving as a wonderful conservation tool? Most definitely. Julie and I wouldn't think of going dove hunting without Maggie and Jet, the black labs, and I can't tell you the number of birds they've found that otherwise would have been lost if it weren't for their assistance. A word of warning, though, for those who take their dogs during the heat of September – WATER. Lots of it. And a shady spot doesn't hurt either.

Dove hunting – the specifics

Although some might disagree, dove hunting is rivaled only by squirrel hunting in its simplicity. Sure, you can try your hand at jump-shooting some mourners during the heat of the day, but for the most part, a dove hunt – a *good* dove

Finding a good dove field isn't always as easy as one might think. Scouting water and food sources, as well as roosting and loafing areas are all keys to success.

Chris Paradise, left, and brother, Rob, assemble and erect the Uncle Greg Version of the Dove Wire. Don't laugh…it works.

hunt now – consists of long periods of sustained shooting broken only by temporary seated lulls designed specifically for eating fruit pies and drinking ice-cold Gatorade. And really, that's about all there is to it. For me, actually putting a dove and my shot pattern in the same place at the same time comprises about 99 percent of the battle; however, for the sake of conversation, let's take a look at a couple particulars that can help you put more doves in your bucket.

The first of these is food. For doves, the quest for food is primarily a morning and evening thing. As for the food source itself – well, that's going to depend on any number of different things, the most significant of which is probably going to be regional; that is, where you're hunting often dictates what the doves will be feeding on, and thus will greatly influence where you will and won't hunt. In much of the Midwest, for instance, that food source will commonly be sunflowers. Often, these fields will have been planted specifically to attract doves, and ultimately, dove hunters. Sunflowers are a popular dove food in the South as well, where again, fields are planted in order to provide hunting opportunities both by attracting birds to a particular location **and** by helping keep birds in the area for an extended period of time.

But sunflowers aren't the only game in town when it comes to doves. Grain eaters, doves are quite fond of small seeded crops such as sorghum, millet, and milo; however, natural plants with similarly small seeds – ragweed and pigweed both immediately come to mind – can also provide excellent hunting, especially if these plants are found in conjunction with relatively open and either sandy or rocky soil.

Which brings me to Point Number Two, something I'll call barren ground. Short-legged things, doves, like woodcock and snipe, aren't big fans of thick, brushy, low-lying cover. Instead, they seem to prefer ground which is more open. Perhaps such ground allows them to get around more easily. Or maybe it has to do with the lack of cover and the bird's ability to readily spot approaching predators. Either way, I've always found my best dove fields to include bare patches of ground – someplace where the birds can walk and pick and walk and pick, which is pretty much all the doves do when they're not flying at Mach 3 or humiliating me.

Point Number Three has direct ties to Point Number One in that whereas doves need feed, they also need a constant supply of water. Water is typically a morning and evening thing – a dove characteristic that hunters can capitalize on simply by locating themselves either at a water source, or at some point between a roost and water, or a mid-day loafing spot and water. It's important to remember that water sources, like food sources, can differ from place to place. Whereas an old quarry pond will work wonders for the hunter in Illinois, the shooter in Texas will be gunning over a stock tank. In Colorado, the hot spot's going to be a sandbar in the middle of the South Platte River, while in eastern Washington, the dove drinks will come courtesy of a small warm-water seep below Potholes Reservoir.

The dove wire up and loaded with Flambeau decoys. Assembly takes but a few minutes. And besides, it's fun to fool with.

Dove wires, dove sticks, etc.

Several years ago, no one knows exactly when, a guy was sitting in a dove field. As he sat, he watched doves landing on an abandoned telegraph line some 100 yards away. He noticed, astute individual that he was, that regardless of where the first dove landed on the wire, the following birds would land alongside. He also noticed that birds which at first seemed hell-bent on over-flying his field often quickly changed direction and – surprise! – lit next to those already perched on the wire. Over time, our guy began to see a pattern. A common denominator, so to speak, until one day while sitting back in his recliner with the Daily News and a cold Pabst Blue Ribbon, the spark burst into flame.

"What if," he thought, "I were to string a wire between to high poles and clip a couple dove decoys to it?" And with that, the doctor smacked the man's idea on the butt and the modern Dove Wire squalled its way into being.

A dove wire? The way I see it, dove hunters flat got tired of feeling left out. After all, duck and goose hunters have their fake birds. Turkey hunters have their decoys. So, too, do those who chase sandhill cranes and crows. Hell, today's outdoor supply catalogs include decoys ranging from whitetail deer to pronghorn antelope, elk, and moose. There's even a spastic rabbit meant to fool coyotes and fox into believing that,

well, this particular entrée has some serious coordination issues. Why not doves?

Enter – the dove wire. In its most basic form, the dove wire consists of little more than a pair of uprights between which is stretched, well, something. Purists wishing to remain true to the dove wire's name often use a cable or rope. Some folks, the Paradise Brothers for instance, opt instead for a run of ½-inch electrical conduit as their perch. Add a couple decoys and a method for keeping the outfit stable and in an upright position, and you're ready to go. Simple? That's the beauty of the dove wire. It *is* simple.

The Paradise Version – Better known as the Uncle Greg Version, named for the Paradise Brothers' Uncle Greg, a very nice gentleman and tech-head who, according to Rob Paradise, lives for designing and building stuff. Greg, says Rob, was the mastermind behind the current version of the brothers' dove wire.

What Greg did was frighteningly simple; however, I must apologize in advance if I don't have the exact measurements correct here. Greg's wire consists of two 10-foot sections of ¾-inch electrical conduit, one 12-foot section of ¾-inch, two two-foot sections of ½-inch conduit, and two 90-degree (¾-inch) elbows. The two 10-footers are the uprights, while the 12-footer with the elbows serves as the cross-member or perch. The two pieces of ½-inch are driven into the ground, and the ends of the 10-footers (Remember…they're ¾-inch, so they fit nicely) fit down

My 10-foot dove stick. Simple and lightweight, it worked well; however, I had more luck combining two units into a 20-foot version. The birds could spot it better.

overtop of them. Done as so, this wire is more than stable, not to mention high enough to catch the eye of any passing birds. A little bit of camouflage duct tape covering the shiny conduit, and the wire's ready for business.

The advantages of Greg's design are many. First, and as already mentioned, it's solid. Secondly, it allows the decoys to be displayed at least 10 feet above the ground, and as all decoy users know, the plastic doves can't work if the birds can't see them. Third, the total cost of wire, excluding the Flambeau dove decoys, had to be less than $15. Fourth, and while the overall length of the rig is 12 feet, it's still relatively easy to transport in a either a pickup or an SUV. NOTE – If you want to go with the Uncle Greg design but are hesitant because the wire won't fit in your Ford Ranger or your Yugo, you can always cut both the 10-footers and the 12-footer in half. Buy yourself three ¾-inch conduit connectors, and assemble the whole thing in the field. Now you're only working with five and six-foot sections instead of 10 and 12-foot.

But to continue. Advantages Five and Six - Greg's wire is lightweight, and can easily be assembled and erected in less than five minutes. And seventh, the damn thing works like a charm. Not every time, but often enough to make a believer out of me. And Julie. And my Pop. And Uncle Greg.

A final note. When Julie and I hunted with the Paradise Brothers, Rob used a few short turns of black electrical tape to secure both the uprights and the crosspiece to the elbows during field assembly. Too, the eight or so Flambeau dove decoys were similarly held tight to their metal perch using the same black electrical tape. Greg mentioned this 'tape' step as somewhat of a side note during our opening day hunt, claiming that an earlier 'untaped' version of the wire allowed the perch *and* the decoys to spin – a characteristic, I'm assuming, the doves found less than attractive.

The Dove Stick – I'm going to mention this one simply because I built one. That, and it seemed to work.

Years ago, I saw what looked like a collapsible television antenna…you know, those constantly busted-up collections of aluminum rods of varying lengths that looked kind of like a Charlie Brown Christmas tree, only shiny? – that came complete with a half-dozen dove decoys. I can't recall for certain, but I think it went by the name of the Dove Tree, or something like that. The theory behind the contraption, I believe, was that the 'tree' could be placed in the ground, the arms raised, and dove decoys placed at random about the metal branches.

Apparently, it stuck with me; however, my version was just a bit different, and consisted of two 10-foot sections of ½-inch conduit, a ½-inch connector, a two-foot piece of ¾-inch conduit, and three four-foot ash branches trimmed neatly…but not too neatly. In the field, I drive the ¾-inch support into the ground. Next, I connect the two 10-footers. One branch is zip-tied tightly a couple inches from the top of the pole. The remaining two branches are zipped together to make one long perch, and this is fastened securely two to three feet below the first. Four or five decoys are clipped to the branches, and the entire rig is hoisted into position and slipped into the larger support conduit. During an Ohio dove hunt in early September of 2002, with the Dove Stick but days old, I watched several birds either land or attempt to land on the ash stick perches. Scientific conclusion? Probably not, but scientific enough to convince at least one goofy dove hunter – me.

A seat in the shade

Say dove hunting, and two stories immediately come to me. The first is from Ohio. Ben Scott, a former student and long-time hunting partner of my father's, found a dove field along the eastern edge of Portage County not far from my folks' home. The good part is that not only did Ben find the field, but he invited me, Julie, and my Pop

Maggie and me on dove patrol in Illinois, one of our favorite places to chase these challenging little gray darts.

The end of another day in the dove fields. Can tomorrow come soon enough for these two?

to come and hunt it. Nice guy, eh?

Anyway, the newly-cut winter wheat field was approximately – I'm guessing – 800 yards long and 250 yards wide. On the north and west sides, there were narrow pin oak and wild cherry treelines. A standing cornfield made up the south side, while the eastern edge was loosely defined by a large alfalfa field. The cut winter wheat was nice; however, the key to this particular field was four huge maple trees in the exact center, all of which sported bare branches in their last 20 or so feet. Any dove entering the airspace above the field made a beeline for one of the maples before settling down to feed, and there must have been hundreds of birds come and go throughout the morning. Despite some problematic shooting, we did well. Particularly my father, who from his seat in the shade underneath one of the maples downed 15 birds – and one Canada goose! – with 22 rounds. Remember the quote from the beginning of this chapter? That originated from this hunt.

The second story takes place in Illinois. Seems that Illinois dove hunters are limited to shooting from noon until 5:00 PM during the first five days of the season. On the sixth day, however, shooting times change to one-half hour before sunrise to one-half hour after. Back in 1999, Julie and I and her youngest son, Robbie, hunted a series of state-owned and managed sunflower fields on Days Four and Five. Oh, we saw a few birds, but nothing to really get excited about.

Day Six rolls around, and we're out in the field before daylight. Still, there's not much to see. 'Round about 4:45, the first doves roll into our little stand of sunflowers. Then a couple more. And a couple more. Relatively new to shotguns and bird hunting, Robbie asks if he can position himself about 100 yards to the south of our stand at a break in the treeline through which he'd watched several birds come and go. After a brief safety reminder, I give him the go-ahead.

It's now 5:05 PM, and somewhere in western Illinois, the dinner bell's ringing and every dove in a dozen counties descends on our field. Only this time instead of grumbling shooters departing a barren field, guns cased and frustratingly clean, they're met with ounce loads of steel #7. From our chairs in the shade, Julie and I join in the excitement. Below us, I watch Robbie shoot. And shoot. And shoot. And occasionally, I watch as he walks out into the stubble to retrieve a dove.

Forty-five minutes go by with hardly a lull. Finally, I look and see Robbie walking in our direction, Remington 11-87 in one hand and a clump of doves in the other. Without a word, he lifts the lid of the cooler and places his birds inside on the newspaper. Then he turns to me, and with a smile on his face, says something that I'll never, ever forget – "M.D.," he asks. "Can I get some more bullets?" It was awesome.

A pair of roosters and a Winchester Model 24 in 16-gauge. Both as much a part of Americana as they come.

6

Kings of the Uplands
Pheasants & Quail

When my English setter, Ike, was a puppy, he would point pheasants from 15 or 20 yards away, freezing at the first whiff of scent and expecting the birds to cower meekly until I flushed them. Pheasants, of course, rarely sit for long (that's why I love wild roosters); they run, they skulk, they hide, they flush wild.

Ike has since learned to point, break, and creep after running birds, but during that first season, he would stop at a distance and I would stomp around in front of him to figure out exactly where the pheasants were, or, for that matter, if they were still there at all.

One afternoon he ran down a fence line and came to a halt, head held high, not really pointing, but not running any more either.

"I think Ike's pointing," I said to my cousin.

"No," said Shaun. "He's just admiring the view."

We had crested a hill overlooking a Grant Wood landscape. Golden cornstalks covered fat, round hills split by a gravel road leading to an iron bridge over the creek. A neat white farmstead sat atop the opposite side of the valley under a blue sky streaked with a few wisps of cloud. That's another reason I love pheasants: they live in beautiful country.

Shaun and I walked past the dog, down to a brush pile at the end of the fence line. Twenty-five birds burst into the air at once, blotting out the tranquil landscape in a flurry of cackles and wingbeats, as if Wood had given up and thrown a glob of bright paints into the middle of the canvas. Recovering in time to shoot, we dropped a rooster apiece from the flock. In a minute it would be time to reload and get after the other birds. First, though, with the long-tailed, copper-feathered bird warm in my hand and the landscape rolling out before me, I made sure I took some time to admire the view.

Phil Bourjaily, shooting editor for Field & Stream, is a wonderful friend and consummate pheasant hunter.

His Honor, the ringneck. Surprising to some, pheasants aren't native to the U.S., nor did they originate in the Midwest pheasant belt, but came via Shanghai, China, and Oregon's Willamette Valley.

Pheasants and pheasant hunting

To me, a kid growing up in northeast Ohio in the early 70s, pheasants and pheasant hunting were a traumatic affair. Why? Well, it was like this. Each year, I would get one – that's one, singular – shot at a – again, singular – rooster pheasant. Despite being the son of a diehard beagle man and spending every Saturday and all holidays beating the brush at places with names like Peck's and Gaston's, Wolfe's and Hillas', it never changed. One rooster, one shot, all year.

Typically, and however unfortunately, I would miss that one shot. Nerves, I figure. Whatever the case, I can remember only a fall or two where I actually made good on my once-annual ringneck opportunity.

I can still remember quite vividly the day I killed my first two-bird limit of wild Ohio roosters. Veterans' Day, 1989. Maybe it was 1990; still, the year wasn't so important as was the fact that I had finally shed my upland hairshirt. No longer could I be called the Jonah of Buckeye State pheasant hunting. I'd done it. Now, it's probably right of me to say here that when I left the state for Washington in October 1993, I hadn't done it again. But still, there was that one glorious day in November when my game vest was heavy, weighted by two of the most wonderful birds I'd ever seen.

Today, Julie and I live in Iowa, more the result of a career-minded fluke than an out-and-out intention. Here in the heart of the Midwest, pheasants are commonplace. Some years, a little more common. And some, a little less; still, there aren't many folks 'round our little town of Martelle – population 280 – who can remember a time when there wasn't at least a few cagey old ringnecks crowing from the springtime cattails. These people grew up with the birds and they've become – well, I guess I'd call it a bit jaded. They've come to expect the sight of a rooster, looking like a live-wired copper penny, strutting his way across a sunlit bean field. To them, he's but a minor distraction on the way to the general store; if, that is, he's noticed at all. But to me, the one-shot-a-year-boy, he's a glorious interruption in what would have otherwise been a lackluster day.

Thank goodness, though, I'm not the only one affected as such. You see, there are folks out there whose world revolves around this gaudy collection of feathers and his earth-tone drab mate. Without the ringneck – without the sounds and the sights and, yes, even the smells, all of which announce the arrival of yet another October – they'd be lost. Homeless. Without direction. Why, without the ringneck pheasant, what would we do all fall? Work?

Drab for a maternal reason, the hen pheasant is the vital element in the creation and proliferation of a hearty wild population.

Courtesy of South Dakota Tourism

A (very) brief history

The ringneck's story here in the United States doesn't begin, as some might assume given today's distribution, in the Midwest, but in the Beaver State of Oregon. Seems that a politician name of Judge Owen Denny, who during the latter stages of the 1800s served as the U.S. Consul-General in Shanghai, China, developed a taste for roast pheasant. Over the next handful of years, Denny made several attempts to ship crates of wild Chinese ringnecks back to his holdings in Oregon's Willamette Valley; however, it wasn't until 1881 that a box of 21 birds finally reached the ground on this side of the Pacific.

And these birds, like the men and women of the time, were survivors. Boy, howdy, did they ever survive. The did so despite the seemingly constant gray and rain that is the western slope of the Cascade Mountain Range. Over the next 35 to 40 years and from these most humble beginnings, the ringneck was introduced into other states. Oregon's sister state to the south, California, received her first birds in 1889. Birds were then shipped to the American West – Utah, Idaho, and Colorado. Texas, Oklahoma, New Mexico, and Arizona came onto the picture around the turn of the century, and were followed by a handful of Midwestern states,

including South Dakota, Ohio, Illinois, and Indiana. Still, this wonderful import was already being touted as the American bird hunter's saving grace. As the westward expansion and the subsequent need to plow, plant, and radically change the habitat had banished the prairie chicken to the environmental back burner, the pheasant continued his march to the East. The Keystone State – Pennsylvania – was next, and in time became one of the country's premier places to hunt wild roosters. And finally, the ringneck made his way up into New England, where during the late 1800s, stockings were undertaken in Massachusetts, Rhode Island, New York, and Maine. Only in the hill country – Kentucky, Tennessee, and the Virginias – and in the American Southeast could the pheasant, save for those instances where the creature was cultivated behind chicken wire and underneath protective netting, be considered an uncommon occurrence.

Today, the ringneck's situation and status is the same yet different. Oregon still has birds; however, most of those can be found not in the Willamette Valley, but in the brushy draws and creek bottoms on the much more arid eastern half of the state. California's population of ringnecks, many say, is spotty and sporadic. "Good years, and not-so-good years" is often the bottom line comment

A pointer holds 'steady' against a backdrop of the Nebraska Sandhills and the machine that pumps the life's blood up the Plains States - water.

the Spring of 2001 that came complete with rain and temperatures well below normal, recorded a harvest of but 470,000 ringnecks during the same period; however, the Hawkeye State, to her defense, had posted four straight (1997-2000) million-plus bird years. At this point, there are those who would be quick to point my obvious omission of both Kansas and Nebraska, states that should by all rights be included in this list of pheasant hunting's best bets. True, both Nebraska and Kansas can provide incredible pheasant hunting, a fact evidenced by The Cornhusker State's 2000 harvest of almost 500,000 birds; however, Mother Nature is putting a strangle hold on pheasant populations in many parts of Nebraska and Kansas in the form of severe drought. "All we need is a little water," the folks in Lincoln and Topeka will tell you. But when will it come? And will it be too late?

Guns and gear for the uplands

Let's get one thing straight first rattle out of the box. Pheasant guns are no different than turkey guns. If you're looking for the ultimate – nay, the perfect – pheasant shotgun – well, friend, you might have a real hard go of it. Are there good pheasant guns? Certainly. The chances are pretty high that there are those shoulder arms that could be considered great pheasant guns. I myself own at least two such *great* pheasant guns. Or I'd like to think so. But perfect? The reality is that few things in life are perfect; however, there definitely is such a beast as close to perfect. And that's what we're going to talk about here.

Shotguns – You choose

Over the years, I've encountered roosters that could have been killed with one of those rubber-tipped suction-cup darts fired from an 8-year-old's all-plastic spring gun. On the other hand, I've also seen birds I know – I know! – couldn't have been brought to bag with an 88-millimeter field artillery piece. Oh, you might hit them, but hitting something and getting something are often two very different things.

Now here's where folks are going to disagree with me, but that's just fine. For I'm going to summarize pheasants and shotguns this way –

Early season ringnecks require killing. Late-season roosters require a lot of killing. And if pheasants, especially tough old cockbirds, were the size of, oh, an emu, we'd never kill one, at least not with a shoulder-fired piece.

heard from hunters in Washington's Yakima Valley and Columbia Basin regions. Montana has its fair share of birds and is a "sleeper" state, according to those who would wish the state remain so. Eastern Colorado also has a fair population of birds. Pennsylvania, unfortunately, isn't what it was 50 years ago. Neither is Ohio, although a man willing to work for his birds might just find one or two old roosters hiding in Pickaway or Fayette counties. New York, Massachusetts and Rhode Island are all in relatively the same proverbial boat with a wild bird here and a wild bird there, but the vast majority of the pheasant hunting opportunities coming courtesy of state-sponsored raise-and-release programs.

Fortunately, pheasant hunters have their salvation in isolated islands of avian Nirvana known as South Dakota and Iowa. In most years, the numbers speak for themselves, such as the 2001 South Dakota pheasant harvest of 1.3 million roosters. Iowa, coming off the Winter of 2000 which saw over 130 consecutive days of snow cover *and*

Pheasants, like turkeys or ducks or whitetails for that matter, have been killed with just about everything conceivable type and size of shotgun known to man. Chris Paradise, the chief public relations and marketing man for O.F. Mossberg & Sons, Inc., shoots a beautiful little over-and-under. The gauge? Actually, caliber is more accurate; for Paradise shoots one of the prettiest little .410 O/Us I've ever seen. **But**, does that make the .410 an across-the-board pheasant gun? I don't think so. On the other end of the spectrum, a gentleman we know here in eastern Iowa guns his roosters with a Browning Citori, chambered for the massive 3½-inch shotshells. This particular over-and-under tips the scales at – and I'm guessing now – right around 42 pounds. Unloaded. Would I want to carry this artillery piece around South Dakota for three days? Only if I could put wheels on it. Still, there are those who would say that the fellow's big gun and big bullets aren't out of place in the uplands, particularly on those late-season days when the roosters flush somewhere 100 yards past wild.

But that still leaves you all waiting on the answer. What is the best pheasant gun? Is it a 3-inch 12? Is it a traditional 2¾-inch chamber? And what about the 20-gauge? And then there are always the 16s. And the 28.

For this particular segment, I decided to go to the one man who I know places shotguns, shotgun shooting, and the ringneck pheasant above everything **except** his wife, his two sons, and his English pointer, Ike. That's the Good Ike, not the occasionally evil, flush-the-pheasants-far-out-of-range, Ike, mind you. The man is Phil Bourjaily, shotgunning editor for *Field & Stream* magazine. What I asked Bourjaily was simple – Rate the gauges.

12-gauge, 3½-inch – "I thought we were talking about pheasant hunting."

12-gauge, 3-inch – "Only with steel, I think."

12-gauge, 2¾-inch – "Yes. It's the standard pheasant gun, especially with the 1¼-ounce high velocity lead loads."

16-gauge – "The 12 is the standard, but then the 16 might even be better if you shoot it in a true, scaled down 16-gauge gun. They always used to say that the 16 gauge carries like a 20-gauge and hits like a 12. That can be true."

20-gauge, 3-inch – "I don't shoot it much, except in steel when I shoot that 3-inch one-ounce steel load."

20-gauge, 2¾ inch – "A fine pheasant gun. Almost what the 16 has. And since most pheasants are killed within 30 yards of the gun, I see no handicap."

A Browning 12, a Winchester Model 24 16-gauge, a Browning 28, and Richard Creason's .410, all tremendous pheasant guns in the proper hands.

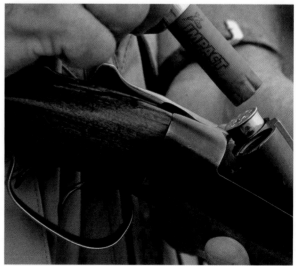

I've had a love affair with the 16-gauge, this M24 in particular, for almost 30 years now. As Phil Bourjaily says - "It's said they carry like a 20 and hit like a 12." I believe it.

Richard Creason went home to central South Dakota with one wish - kill a rooster with his Grandmother's Savage .410 single shot. He killed two.

28-gauge – "Getting light for pheasants, but I have killed wild pheasants with it using a ³/₄-ounce load of #7½ shot. If you're going to buy a gun specifically for pheasant hunting, I wouldn't say buy a 28; however, it will kill wild birds."

.410 bore – "I have friends that shoot them at pheasants. I never would. It's a little gun. It doesn't have many pellets, and it doesn't pattern very well."

My personal story in regards to pheasant guns has been one of chronological change. As I've gotten older and perhaps a bit wiser – no laughing! – my choice of shotguns for pheasant hunting has changed from one of heavy game bags through superior firepower to thinking I'll be a bit more selective in the shots that I take and a bit more strategic in my hunting tactics. This way, I can leave the engraved telephone pole in the gun cabinet and instead shoulder either a Browning Citori Lightning Feather 20-

gauge O/U weighing 5.7 pounds, or a Winchester Model 24 16-gauge side-by-side that tips the scales at a mere 6.4 pounds. Both are a joy to carry all day, and when combined with the proper ammunition – more on that below – they're both potent pheasant medicine.

A word on ammunition

Strict wasn't the word for the guy, but then again, I wouldn't have expected anything else out of a former Navy pilot and retired Northwest Airlines captain. "We're not going to shoot at birds on the ground. Not even cripples. That's why we have dogs. And we're not going to shoot at birds on the level. And we're not going to carry our firearms in an unsafe manner," he stated, leaving no room for discussion. "And finally, if you're shooting those cheap $2.99 a box field loads, leave 'em here. I have good shells I'll sell you. I don't like wounded birds, and cheap shells make for cripples. Now, wadaya say, let's go enjoy ourselves." As I made for the door, I could see a couple of orange-clad figures, heads lowered, reaching for their wallets. "Yep," I could hear the old flyer's voice as it drifted out into the drive. "The best bullets money can buy. Thanks."

I have to admit that while the old man was opinionated and gruff, he was nonetheless correct in his views concerning pheasants and cheap ammunition. Why, he reminded his group of hunters, would you pay $150 a day to hunt pheasants on his ground, and Lord knows how much on your hotel, food, fuel, beer, and other things, and then turn around and buy the cheapest ammunition available? "It just doesn't make any sense, now does it?" he summarized. Well, there's no arguing with thinking like that.

And the old man's right. It doesn't make any sense to go to the effort to find and corner a cagey old rooster, only to insult him and frustrate yourself by touching off three rounds better suited for close-in field mice and English sparrows. Here again, I turned to Bourjaily and his views on what constitutes some of the finer shot size choices when it comes to handling these often-fickle birds.

#4 – "I don't shoot them simply because it takes a pretty heavy payload to cram enough pellets into a shotshell to use them for pheasants. I think you'd probably have to shoot the short magnums (2³/₄-inch, 1½- or 1⅝-ounce loads) to make the most of #4s, and I just never do. It can, however, be a great late-season load, or if you hunt in one of those great big gang hunts where there are birds flying off in all directions and all angles and at all distances."

#5 – "Number 5s are great. I have shot them pretty

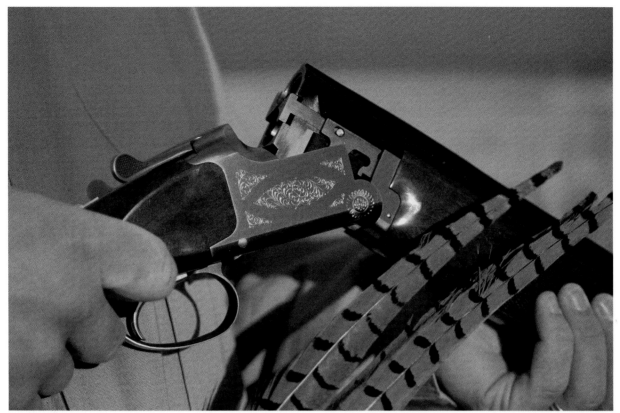

Number 6 shot performs well in this Citori 20-gauge; however, it's not the only choice available to pheasant hunters, and not the only choice that works well.

much all season long. They're great pellets when you need to kill longer-range, going-away birds. Winchester's #5 high-velocity load is just tremendous."

#6 – "I think is the standard, all-round shot size for pheasants. I mean; you can't ever really go wrong with them. This is especially true in the 20-gauge where you only have an ounce of shot to deal with. In the 12-gauge, the 1¼-ounce load is great, though you have to be careful not to shoot your birds too close as it'll put a lot of pellets in them. They're pretty consistent out to 40 yards, and they'll pretty much do everything you want them to do."

#7½ – "I've shot them a lot. People say they're too light. I would disagree. And these haven't all been shots over pointing dogs, either. To me, either a 1⅛ or 1¼ ounce of #7½ works very well. I would probably err toward bigger shot for pheasants. I don't necessarily believe in *early-season* and *late-season* loads for pheasants. In my experience, birds will be in your face one day, then flushing at long range the next, only to be back in your face the next. And if I try to guess whether they'll be close or far? I'm never right. You know, the ones that are far are generally too far to shoot at regardless of what shot size you're shooting."

#8 and beyond – "No."

Another word on ammunition

Until now, when I've mentioned ammunition choices – shot sizes, specifically – I'm been referring to traditional lead shot loads; however, I'd certainly be remiss if I didn't speak briefly on non-toxic shotshells. Why would I be remiss? Two reasons really. First, there are those places where bird hunters are required by state mandate to use nothing *but* non-toxic shotshells on public land. South Dakota's one. And there's some in Iowa and Washington State. Also, many National Wildlife Refuges require non-toxic shot for upland hunting. If you look around, you may find many, many more.

The second reason is also simple – they work. Today's steel shotshells are a far cry from the less-than-stellar choices we were offered back in the early 1990s. And not only are these steel shotshells better performers, but they're also less costly and much more widely varied in terms of shot sizes and charges than were their predecessors.

But steel isn't the only choice available to the upland hunter who finds himself either mandated or choosing to use non-toxic ammunition. Today, these choices include metallurgic concoctions with names like bismuth and tungsten, matrix and polymer. And Hevi-Shot. Let's not forget that. Each performs well in its own right, and each has its place, both in the field and in the wallet. Here, the

Outdoor writer Berdette Zastrow (left) and my wife and photographer, Julie, both agree on the merits of protective - and tough - canvas or oil-cloth brush pants for the uplands.

briefest of run-downs might look like this –

Remington's Hevi-Shot - A mixture of oddly-shaped pellets comprised of 50 percent tungsten, 35 percent nickel, and 15 percent iron. Hevi-Shot's claim to fame rests on the statement that it's denser than lead, which it is – lead's 11.2 grams per cubic centimeter versus 12 grams per for Hevi-Shot (HS). Available in #4 through #7.5 shot, and a 2¾-inch, 12-gauge load of #9 shot. Personally, Hevi-Shot can be used for everything from geese to grouse, and its nothing short of extraordinary. The downside, if there is one? Cost. At this printing Hevi-Shot costs from $1.75 to $2 per bullet. For the cost-conscious, Remington also offers a fine inexpensive steel shotshell known as *Sportsman Steel* – a good bargain bullet; 2¾ -inch in #4, 6, & 7 shot, and in 20-gauge #7.

The Federal Cartridge Company (www.federalcartridge.com) – Federal offers hunters a choice of metallurgic combinations including tungsten-polymer, tungsten-iron, and tungsten-iron/steel in various hull lengths and shot sizes.

The Bismuth Cartridge Company (www.bismuth-notox.com) – Next to lead on the periodic table of ele-

ments, bismuth provides a much heavier alternative than does steel, the shot being comprised of 97 percent bismuth and 3 percent tin. Interesting to note is the fact that The Bismuth Cartridge Company is the only outfit building non-toxic loads for the country's 28 and .410 shooters. The company's upland options include a *Sporting Game Load*, available in 12, 16, 20, 28, & .410, and in shot sizes #4 to 7½, and a *Magnum buffered game load* in 12 and 20-gauge; shot sizes #4, 5 and 6.

Kent Cartridge Company (www. kentgamebore.com) – Makers of IMPACT tungsten-matrix. The 'matrix' simply means a mixture of powdered tungsten and polymers, or nylon, in amounts designed to approximate lead in density and performance. I shot IMPACT #6 – Kent does make a fine 2¾-inch 1⅜-ounce load of #5 in the tungsten-matrix as well – out of my father's 1952 Winchester Model 24 16-gauge double during the whole of the 2002-2003 pheasant season, and was incredibly impressed with the performance. Which reminds me: For those of you shooting older guns, bismuth and Kent's IMPACT are as kind to the firearms are they are deadly on the feathered quarry in front of them.

And, steel – Those are the 'exotic' non-toxics, but for those of you restricted to and searching for a non-lead alternative whose properties aren't that of an alchemist's dream and the price of which is a bit more reasonable than $1.75 per round – well, there's always steel. Today, each of the major players in the ammunition industry, including Remington, Federal, Kent and Winchester, manufacture a variety of outstanding steel shot loads, many of which will work just fine for ringnecks and bobwhites. As for shot size with steel, I believe I'll defer to the waterfowler's rule of thumb: Use two shot sizes larger in steel than you would traditionally use in lead. That said, I'd suggest 1⅛- or 1¼-ounce #3 or #4 steel for those chasing roosters, and Winchester's one-ounce loads of steel #7s for smaller upland birds such as quail, snipe, and doves.

The well-dressed pheasant hunter

Disreputable. Casual. Formal. Any of these three can describe today's pheasant hunter in terms of dress. Go to a fancy shooting preserve – Greystone Castle in Texas, Idaho's Flying B Ranch, or the famed Paul Nelson Farm in South Dakota – and your Levi's, flannel shirt with the torn pocket, and knee-high rubber mud boots might be met with more than one…well, let's just say that the glances will be less than admiring. Still, I've killed many pheasants dressed just as described above and I'm perfectly fine with that.

That said, let's take a brief look at several different elements of dress, remembering that these suggestions can apply not only to pheasants, but to any type of upland hunting, including rabbits and the like.

Pants – You can spend $40 on a pair of Wrangler – The jeans people – brush pants, or you can drop $120 on a set of Oil Finish Tin Cloth Double Hunting Pants from Filson. I use them both, and recommend each highly; however, there are a ton of varieties, makes, and models out there, any one of which may work very well for your pheasant hunting needs. I will say this as you prepare to make your choice – You get what you pay for.

Shirts –Typically, I want something long-sleeved, even during the early season when it's warm, simply for the protection that long sleeves provide. This year, I discovered the Sharptail, a very nice middleweight shirt from Columbia which features blaze orange on the forearms and shoulders. Alone, it makes for a great warm weather garment; however, when I face cooler temperatures, I've taken to wearing the shirt over a wool military sweater. That particular combination is warm and very comfortable, yet not so bulky that it impairs my shooting.

Coats – Over the past few years, I've gradually dropped the hunting coat from my pheasant gear almost completely. Why? Well, with today's synthetics, wools, and other blends, the heavy Carhartt canvas coat of yesterday just isn't necessary. Today, I'll layer, and top everything off with a well-worn game vest. Only on the coldest of days, when the wind howls and everyone with an ounce of intelligence is huddled around the woodstove, will I wear a canvas coat.

Boots – The pheasant hunter, like the infantryman, lives by his feet. So footwear, whatever the style, is a priority. Essentially, there are two choices – leather, and synthetics. If you don't mind the care involved in maintaining a good leather boot, and by care I'm speaking of periodic cleaning, conditioning, and waterproofing, then I'd suggest a lightweight leather boot in either the short, Chukka-style upper, or the traditional 7- to 8-inch upper. Myself, I'm partial to a mix of synthetics. Regardless of the make and model, the key to keeping your feet happy in the field is simple – Get something that fits.

Vests – For the past three or four seasons, I've worn what I'll call a traditional style vest from the folks at Filson, a heavy oil cloth version with ample pocket space, blaze orange chest patches, and a roomy game bag. Julie, on the hand, wears a simpler shoulder-strapped game bag, which features an adjustable belt buckle closure and a blaze orange back. Both serve the purpose of carrying things into and out of the field.

My God, that's an incredible picture! Oh, yeah…the vest. Get yourself a good vest.

Rooster strategies

Here's the most elemental statement I can make when it comes to discussing the ringneck pheasant and hunting strategies. There is nothing – NO THING – that a rooster doesn't know about the art of escape and evasion. He'll sit when he should fly. And he'll fly when he should sit. He'll run to the edge of the earth, and then fly off, cackling, a speck on the horizon. He can hide behind a toothpick, and burrow into things meant only for badgers and cave explorers. The ringneck pheasant's middle name is *frustration*. And we absolutely love him for it.

Opening Day – Ah, opening day. Here some may disagree, but I'm going to call the opening day of pheasant season both a joy and a bearer of false promise. A strange description, perhaps, but I have my reasons. You see, opening day – any opening day for that matter – is a time of renewal. For pheasant hunters in the Midwest, it's a time, an excuse really, to visit with friends and family. A time to call in sick or to relax and laugh – a sort of pre-Thanksgiving, I guess you could say. More often than not, opening day brings with it success.

Opening day can mean drab, first-year roosters and gaudy cocks both. It's a good idea to look sharp, and then look again, before pressing the trigger.

The author in typical thick Iowa pheasant cover. Opening day lasts but a few hours. The rest of the season - well, this is where the birds will be.

Nobby-spurred roosters, just into their first white collar. Year-old cocks, senses perhaps dulled by the recent nine-month reprieve holding tight but inches from the quivering pup's nose. It's good shots, bad shots, and plenty of shooting all around. You'll usually end up with hefty game bags, nice weather, and some much-needed exercise. All in all, opening day is a good thing. And then, reality sets in. Think about 14 inches of snow and December wind chills well below zero. Imagine 100-yard flushes and birds that start running even as you think – "You know. I should go pheasant hunt today." After a while, you begin to think of yourself as less of a pheasant hunter, and more of a life support system for the Model 1100 you've been toting – unfired – for…what's it been, a week now? Ah, how it changes. Opening day is like running the kick-off back for a touchdown. But the rest of the season is that long drive for the score. And that truly separates the pheasant chasers from the pheasant hunters.

The rest of the season – It's true. Everything **does** change immediately after opening day. In fact, it's always amazed me just how quickly pheasants –

roosters and hens alike – learn to associate the sound of truck doors and the hollow thunk-thunk of shotshells being dropped into over/under tubes with danger. Maybe I'm giving them too much credit. Maybe it's nothing more than the fact that the less fortunate roosters – I refuse to call them dumb – get to go home with folks on opening day. And what happens to the survivors? Well, they survived for one reason or another. Luck could certainly have played in their continued existence; still, if even 50 percent of the roosters that survived the opening day onslaught did so simply out of luck, then doesn't that leave 50 percent that might just have figured out this orange-clad, canine-calling process? And if that's the case, then those are the birds I'm here to talk to you about. Certainly, you're going to find what I'll call opening day birds throughout the rest of the season. And sometimes you're just going to have to turn your head skyward and send up a note of thanks for the bird you just got – like the wickedly long-spurred old rooster that my father and I killed one mid-December morning after we caught the bird cackling at the top of his little pheasant lungs in a tiny patch of foxtail, He screwed up. This time, he wasn't lucky; we were. What I'm trying to say here is that post-

Opening Day pheasants are anything but easy; however, there are certain strategies that we hunters can employ which can take at least a little bit of the frustration out of the mix. And as for luck? Don't ever disregard this often-maligned factor. Hell, when it comes to a late-season ringneck, I'd much rather be lucky than smart or good. There's more consistency in it.

Going one-on-one – I'm not trying to be anti-social here, but after opening day, I'd much rather hunt roosters solo than in a group. Okay, maybe two of us, but that's going to about be my limit. Why alone? For starters, I'm going to be quieter by myself. Now that's not to say there won't be the occasional conversation with one or both of the black labs, but overall, I'm going to hunt much more quietly when I only have myself to worry about. This means no slamming truck doors or tailgates, and no slamming bolts. No talking and no discussions on how to approach a particular piece of cover. Alone, I seem to be more thorough in my dissection of a parcel, a topic I'll talk about here in just a minute.

Think of solo pheasant hunting as a small covert operations team making a surgical strike on an enemy encampment. The objective? Get your team in quietly, retrieve the information, and get out quietly without anyone knowing that anything was amiss. Melodramatic? Perhaps, but it works for me…especially in the late-season.

Now, right away I'm going to try to address the popular thought that the solo pheasant hunter is at a disadvantage, simply because he can't cover enough ground nor can he cover that ground effectively. Factor in that this lone hunter has no dog, and most would be quick to consider such an outing a waste of time. Opposite thinker that I am, I view hunting alone as an advantage. A couple reasons –

1. The lone hunter is forced to dissect larger parcels of ground into smaller, more manageable sections. This accomplishes two things. First, it makes the hunter high-grade the area he's going to hunt; that is, he studies the ground more carefully in order to decide which five or six one-acre sections to hunt rather than trying to blunder through the entire 100 acres without a plan or a purpose. And secondly, the soloist soon learns that strategy does indeed play a key role in success. He takes his time, and decides how each of these one-acre sections he's cut from the rest would best be hunted. He knows that in many cases, a rooster has to run out of running room before he's going to fly. Knowing this, he determines that Section 1 should be pushed from north to south, or toward a cut beanfield. Section 2, on the other hand, needs to be run from east to west where a wide, shallow slough will serve as a barrier. And so on and so on

When working large blocks of cover - the property shown consists of 101 acres of CRP ground - the lone gunner needs to cut the cover into manageable pieces.

and so on. In summary – Cut your ground into pieces, and then work the sections toward some type of cover break. Running willy-nilly through the puckerbrush…well, that's just not going to get it.

2. I've found that when I'm hunting alone, I work the cover more slowly and thus more thoroughly. Once I've decided where I'm going to hunt and determined my strategy, I'll typically start working into the wind because any noise I inadvertently make will be blown behind me, and any birds flushed will usually jump into the wind before hooking back with the breeze in their tail feathers. As I hunt, I'll work back and forth, back and forth, zigzagging through the cover, stopping often just so as to make any would-be sit-tight rooster think that I've seen him and am preparing to pounce. I might, you never know. Each time I stop, I try to mentally prepare myself for a flush. Each time I reach a cover break, regardless how small or seemingly insignificant, I again prepare myself. Looking back, and while I don't have any concrete numbers to support my claim, I'd feel very safe in saying that at least 75 percent of the roosters I've jumped while

No dog, no dice? No way. This old rooster came during a one-on-one hunt in eastern Iowa. In November. It's not easy, but it can be done.

then getting Jet, Julie's lab, in February of 1999, when I haven't hunted with the help of a dog; HOWEVER, that's certainly not to say that the soloist sans hound can't kill birds.

Maybe he'll have to downsize his parcels even more. Maybe he'll have to zig-zag-and-stop a little more often. Or perhaps he needs to be in the field right at legal shooting time – a strategy I call *Catch 'em before they're fully awake*. The dog-free hunter should consider heading afield when the wind's howling and the birds are concentrated and when the snow's deep and the walking's tough. There's nothing even remotely easy about hunting ringnecks by yourself without a dog, but then again, there was nothing simple about bringing Apollo 13 safely back to Earth, now was there? And that was done. NOTE – To the dogless hunter: Birds that are hit need to be marked quickly and carefully, and it's important that you get there immediately! Unless you're going to kill both birds stone dead, there's no sense in shooting a double and only finding one. *If* a bird falls and gets to his feet *and* the cover and safety permits, shoot him again. Do not hesitate. And for God's sake, don't live under the illusion that you'll run him down. You won't.

Walkers and blockers – Today, it seems as if the hunt-and-peck method of pheasant hunting – the one or two folks looking here and walking there – is slowly being replaced by a kind of deer-drive strategy; that is, X number of hunters stand while Y number walk in their general direction. The goal or objective here is to use the standers as a sort of human cover break. Any birds that run – meaning 95 percent of the roosters in any given parcel – will eventually, it's hoped, end up against this wall of humanity where they have nothing else left in their bag 'o tricks except for one final maneuver – flight. Some times it works, and works well. Other times, it doesn't. However, this technique known as blocking, or as it's sometimes referred to as *walkers and blockers*, is being used across the country so much so that in some locales, blocking has damn near replaced walking as the primary method of producing limits of birds. Why do it? Why is it effective? Are there any right or wrong ways to go about using this strategy? I'll take these one at a time now.

hunting alone have flushed while I was standing still. Seems that *rustle-rustle-shuffle-SILENCE* cadence makes them awful nervous. And one last note here. Overlook nothing; that is, there is no such thing as an insignificant patch of fill-in-the-blank when it comes serving as a rooster's hideout. I won't, but I could go on at length about the old bird I found in the 20-foot-square clump of cattails in Gary Robertson's picked beanfield. Or the half dozen roosters that flushed from the Buick-sized thicket of hedge trees and brome grass on Jim Barber's place. Believe me, roosters live in these forgotten coverts for the same reason that 180-class whitetails live there…no one goes there. Make sure you do.

3. And finally – what about the hunter going one-on-one *without*? Without a dog, that is? Well, to tell you the truth, I can't remember the time since bringing Maggie, our oldest black lab, to Iowa in 1997, and

1. Why – This one's relatively simple to explain. Pheasants, in many cases and under a wide variety of conditions, would rather run than fly. Deep snow, wet weather, or hip-crunching heavy cover will often translate into roosters that would rather squat and hope you hurry by them. It is something that happens very, very frequently. Believe me. Thin cover, however, such as early season brome grass or standing corn, more often than not, sets the stage for

Here, the author and Jet prepare to push a small weedy field toward standers a short distance to the east...and out of the picture.

extended bouts of avian running. Birds that run and refuse to fly are therefore safe, unless you're hunting with one of the old-schoolers like my Father who subscribes to the theory of – "If he's going to run like a rabbit, I'm going to shoot him like a rabbit." To each his or her own, I'm fond of saying. The bottom line is this. You block to stop the running, and force birds into the air.

2. Why is it effective – The truth of the matter is blocking is only effective 50 percent of the time; that is, it either works or it doesn't. But just *why* does it work when it does? Well, it's no different than a slow, methodical push through an area of cover toward a cover break. Here, however, instead of the aforementioned cover break to help force birds into the air, you're using shooters.

3. The right way and the wrong way – Is there really a right and wrong way to stand and block? Well, after serving as both walker and blocker in some of the country's premier pheasant country, I can honestly say that I have learned this much about the tactic –

a. When possible, bite off smaller chunks of the entire property, and try to walk-and-block these first. The smaller the parcel, the more completely it can be covered, both by the movers and by the shooters.

In some cases – a South Dakota cornfield or 80 acres of uninterrupted switchgrass – well, you're just going to have to play with the cards you're dealt there. In such large-scale situations, it can help to place what I'll call moving-shooters slightly ahead and to the sides of the line of walkers. These folks will hopefully catch those roosters that attempt to squirt out the sides. There are some case-specific safety considerations here, things we'll discuss in just a moment.

b. Make certain your walkers run the cover *completely* to the end. And I'm talking about the very last couple of inches. So thoroughly that the walkers and the blockers can shake hands once that particular push is over. Remember – a rooster pheasant can hide behind a goldenrod stem. If you leave him with someplace to hide, he'll hide there. If you leave him an *OUT*, he'll take full advantage of it. And you.

c. Stealth, quiet, and coordination all play vital roles in the success or failure of any push. As a stander, you should get into position quietly – no bolt slamming, no talking to your buddy, no yelling at the dog – and you should be given enough time to get into position and get ready before the push begins. Believe it or not, pheasants aren't on the same page as those who would shoot them; that is,

Ohio's Bob "Oly" Olsen with a canine partner and a beautiful Nebraska rooster.

On canine assistance

On canine assistance – I may not be the sharpest tool in the shed, but I do know enough not to enter into an argument with a man about the qualifications – or lack thereof – of his bird dog any more than I'd criticize his choice in whiskey or shotguns. Why? Because it's a no-win situation…and it probably should be.

Let me just say this about pheasants and dogs. Introducing a canine assistant onto the upland playing field transforms the event from a sandlot ball game to a full-fledged under-the-lights major league deal. Basically, it's night and day. A good dog is an asset unmatched in the realm of the pheasant hunter. With him or her, you'll find more birds, retrieve more cripples, and without question enjoy yourself more than you ever thought possible.

I'm not going to provide lots of in-depth coverage here; however, what I'd like to do is to take a quick look at some of the breeds most commonly seen in the pheasant fields. I won't select nor comment on good or bad, better or best. Those are your decisions, not mine. The only division I will make concerns pointing dogs, those are the ones that will wait for you, and the flushing breeds, otherwise known as the ones you better keep up with. And with that, the pointing dogs -

English pointer – My research shows the English pointer going back to the mid-17th century, with upbringings primarily in England but with roots in Spain. This dog is a favorite among upland bird hunters nationwide.

English setter – Hunting partner, Phil Bourjaily's, dog, Ike, is an English setter, and a quite skilled one at that. I've found them to be wonderful dogs, though a bit independent, and prone to drooling on your pheasants rather than retrieving them.

Brittany spaniel – Wrap pure energy up in a furry, liver-and-white bundle, and you'd have created a Brittany spaniel. Introduced to America in the 1930s, the Brittany is the only pointing spaniel.

German shorthair pointer – As the name implies, this pointer has roots in the Fatherland dating back to the late 1800s; however, it wasn't seen in the states until early in the 20th century. Originally bred as an all-round hunter, the GSP has grown in popularity among the nation's pheasant fanatics.

Vizsla – A short-haired pointer of Hungarian descent. It's pronounced *vees-la*.

Weimaraner – Another German, the Weimaraner was originally bred as a big game hunter; however, with the lack of roe deer in the United States,

they're not always going to wait until you're ready before they start boiling out…right in front of where you should have been standing. Walkers? They need to move slowly, and work the cover thoroughly. Oh, and there's no need to be talking or yelling back and forth, other than what's necessary for keeping everyone in line. Believe me, your presence is noise enough.

d. And finally, a couple notes on safety. First, every push should have a coordinator – someone who knows the ground and the routine. This person is King, and his or her word is final. It's a safety issue. Next, everyone should be wearing a blaze orange cap **and** some type of blaze orange on their upper chest or shoulders – minimum. Stay in line. Think about it. Do you really want to walk through head-high corn, 35 feet in front of six guys with guns…even if they are your friends? It's common sense. Here, talk back and forth enough so that you maintain a straight line. Then there's the *no low shooting* rule. EVERY shot is up – some say no less than 45 degrees – and away from the lines of both walkers and blockers. And finally, blockers. When the King says, "Stand there," you just stand there. Moving 40 yards one side or the other can be hazardous to your well-being..

There are few things better than teaming up with a capable companion, and this little South Dakota spaniel was as capable as they come.

Richard Kieffer and Ebony, a wonderful black lab dog that loved nothing more than finding roosters and giving "kisses."

uplanders soon found something other for the Deutsch dog to chase.

German wirehair pointer – Introduced to America around 1920, the GWP is recognized for its multi-tasking capabilities; that is, as a pointer, a water retriever, and as an accomplished fetcher of rabbits and hares.

And now the flushing breeds –

Labrador retriever – I love labs! Extremely intelligent, labs make great all-round hunters and fantastic pets for all ages, though their size and enthusiasm can from time to time prove frustrating should you decide to keep one indoors. An interesting note – The first recorded birth of a Labrador in a shade other than black was a yellow pup born in 1899. Today, three flavors exist – black, yellow, and chocolate.

Golden retriever – A tremendously friendly dog, and a right good pheasant hound. Goldens were developed in the late 19th century, and today are recognized as one of nation's most versatile breeds, with members serving in Search & Rescue operations, and as guide dogs for the blind and physically challenged.

English springer spaniel – Like the Brittany, the springer is a bundle of energy, and an excellent pheasant dog; however, he might be a bit high-strung for some tastes.

I know some will think what I'm about to say might seem like blasphemy, yet here I go. Any dog, regardless of breed, that will put a rooster into the air within acceptable gunning range and make a reasonable attempt to retrieve a downed bird can be called a pheasant dog. At least that's the way I see it. Over the years, I've enjoyed the company of some fine non-traditional bird dogs, including beagles, bassets, Irish setters, collies, and a wonderful black lab/pit bull Heinz-57 type that was one of the hardest-working dogs I've ever seen. Each found pheasants – alive and dead – and each enjoyed a scratch behind the ears, a rub on the belly, and every single morsel of Moon Pie they could get their lips around. Now I ask you. Do you really need anything more than that?

I should mention a couple final notes on the subjects of rooster spurs and dispatching cripples. Spurs, especially the razor-sharp dueling spurs of older birds, can cut you, badly. And while these injuries are most commonly the result of foolishly leg-grabbing crippled yet very lively birds, the spurs on dead roosters are also certainly capable of causing a nasty cut or two.

As far as dispatching cripples, here's one I learned long ago. Hold the bird by the chest in both hands, your hands side by side. Center your fingers at and slightly behind (tail-ward) the point where the wing meets the

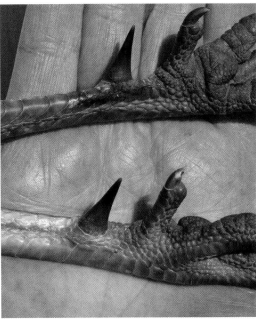
Think it'll hurt when he runs these through your palm? He has them for a reason. Oh, and yes. It will hurt.

body. Your thumbs should be positioned directly opposite your fingers. Now squeeze. This method compresses the bird's lungs and heart, and typically causes death within 20-30 seconds, an end usually signaled by a final flutter of the rooster's wings. The Squeeze Technique not only works quickly, but it keeps your bird looking nice should you decide to stop by your local taxidermy studio on the way home. That, and it's much more respectful than grabbing him by the head and whipping him around like a dishrag, now isn't it?

Hunting Gentleman Bob and his buddies

The United States is blessed with several very different species of quail. Mostly, these differences are in distribution, voice, and appearance. But some have a completely different attitude, like the scaled quail of the Southwest. These birds live to run and would rather scamper a mile over broken rock and cactus, than fly even 20 yards. This can necessitate a change in hunting techniques, and even equipment. For now, let's take a look at the principle players, a family known simply as quail –

Bobwhites – For many hunters living in the eastern United States, the bobwhite quail ranks as *the* upland game bird, for in him is held decades of tradition, history, and heritage. Hunted by Presidents and eaten by kings, the bobwhite symbolizes some of the finest that wild America has to offer. Today, it's said that the largest numbers of wild bobwhites can be found in Texas. And while that may be true, Gentleman Bob's holding his own throughout much of the Midwest – Iowa, Kansas, and

Illinois, to name a few – and in the Southeast, most notably in Georgia, Virginia, and the Carolinas. Smaller populations of bobwhites can be found in the Pacific Northwest, as well as in the foothills of the Rocky Mountains.

Bobwhites are plump birds, weighing 7 to 8 ounces. Coloration is a mottled collection of browns, tans, buffs, blacks, and whites. Facial markings on the cocks are white, while those of the hens is a pretty yellow-buff color.

Those specifically seeking bobwhites almost always accompany themselves with one of the pointing breeds; however, the dog-free hunter can find success by concentrating on either early morning feeding or mid-afternoon loafing areas. For whatever reason – and I'm going to venture a guess it has to do with protection from aerial predators – bobwhites seem to prefer some overhead cover, particularly woody cover. Knowing this, hunters may want to begin their search where such food sources and overhead cover are intermingled – where a brushy woodlot adjoins a harvested corn or soybean field, for instance. At the covey rise, it's vital to concentrate on one bird. Resist the urge to flock-shoot. Once scattered, single bobwhites often have a tendency to embed themselves in cover tighter than a beggar tick in a wool blanket. After the rise, try to mark the singles well. Then, take your time, and if hunting with a dog, trust his or her nose.

Valley quail – The state bird of California, this Western game bird is also known – surprise! – as the California quail. Valley quail are birds of the West Coast, ranging from Baja California in the south to British Columbia in the north. Today, excellent populations can be found in eastern Washington along the Columbia, Yakima, and Snake rivers as well as in central and eastern Oregon.

Six ounces is about as much as a valley quail will weigh. The most noticeable difference between these quail and bobwhites is a plume or topknot worn by both sexes…yes, just like that cartoon quail in the old Warner Brothers pictures. The male's plume is jet-black, while the hen's is a lighter brown or buff. Cock valley quail have white facial streaks, a black throat, and heavily barred sides; hens are a mixture of subdued browns and blacks.

Hunting California quail in Washington's Yakima Valley or the foothills of the Blue Mountains is like hunting bobwhites in Kansas; that is, food and water are key items or starting points. Cover, be it wheat stubble in the early season or the thicker grasses found alongside irrigation canals during late October and into November, can be hunted depending upon the time of year and weather conditions. A good pointing dog can be a bonus, particularly in the more open terrain as is found in eastern Oregon where these birds show no hesitancy to run instead of hide.

With his round figure and bright white facial markings, the cock bobwhite is easy to identify.

A tremendous photograph of a pair of valley (California) quail. Notice the black plume or topknot, a very distinctive feature of the fascinating western species.

Those seeking an audience with bobwhites, regularly use dogs, often pointers but occasionally flushers. The same is true when hunting most of the quail species found in the U.S.

Gambel's quail – Also known as the desert quail. He makes his home in the American Southwest – Texas and New Mexico, as well as in southern California, Utah, Nevada, Colorado, and portions of Idaho. Hawaii, too, has Gambel's quail…or more precisely, Hawaii's island of Lanai has Gambel's. Mesquite and cactus are all the cover they need; however, in recent years, drought and the all-too-common human encroachment, even into the desert, has precipitated a fall in Gambel's populations.

Gambel's quail are quite similar in appearance to their California cousin – topknot, barred sides, and 5 to 6 ounces in weight. The Gambel's cock does differ in his rusty-red head crown and a very distinctive black patch on his off-white chest and lower portions.

Put on your track shoes 'cause these birds would much rather run than fly. The singles and doubles, I'm told, hold much better than do the often wide-flushing coveys. That said, you might want to consider adding a couple jugs of water and an oxygen bottle to your desert quail hunting gear. Pointing dogs can help, but take pains to properly prepare your pointer for the often-hostile environment of the American desert. This means dog booties, your Leatherman pliers, and some pre-season snake-proofing.

Scaled quail – These birds are also known as blue quail, cottontops and blue racers. Whatever you call them, scaled quail make their home in the American

Southwest, primarily in portions of New Mexico and Arizona; however, birds can also be found in West Texas, with lesser numbers in southwestern Kansas and the Oklahoma Panhandle.

The scaled quail gets its name from the scale-like feather patterns which cover the bird's neck, chest, and underparts. The back, as well as parts of the neck and upper chest, shows a light grayish-blue; hence, the *blue quail* handle. Both sexes are visually similar, right down to the trademark white-topped crest or crown.

Again, I'm going to refer to the track shoes and oxygen bottle strategy as blues would much rather run than fly. A Hoover-nosed pointing dog certainly can help. So, too, can a "Get in front of them and head 'em off…or try" tactic. Either way, hunting scalies means running.

Mountain and Mearn's quail –

The mountain quail, North America's largest at 8 or 9 ounces and often 12 inches from beak to tail, can be found throughout the Pacific Northwest, and in parts of New Mexico, Nevada, and California, where it spends most of its time in higher elevations among scrub oaks and buck brush cover. The Mearn's quail, also known as the Montezuma or Harlequin quail due to its unusual coloration, is another inhabitant of the Southwest, with the highest numbers found in Mexico, South Texas, and southern Arizona.

Mountain quail and Gambel's look very similar, sharing the black throat patch, slate-gray back and upper chest, and heavily barred sides. The main difference between the two is where the Gambels' topknot is a distinctive forward-curving plume, the mountain quail's head gear is straight or curves slightly rearward. The hen Mearn's resembles the familiar female bobwhite. The cock, however, is a mottled mix of browns and blacks, with a dash of gray, white, and rust; that is, except for his face, which is a mask of vivid white markings on a background of dark bluish-black. These unique facial markings have earned the Mearn's the nickname "*masked quail.*"

Mountain quail are migratory; that is, within their own small home range. Early season – September or October – will find them at higher elevations among the oaks, but as autumn gives way to winter, the birds will wander down lower where they'll often be found with valley quail. Here, they're hunted in much the same way as are California quail, or bobwhites, for that matter. Mearn's are seldom hunted specifically. Rather, they're sometimes taken as incidentals by those seeking desert (Gambel's) or scaled quail.

Chukars – It's unfortunate, but my only experience thus far with chukars has come courtesy of any number of shooting preserves. On such facilities, these fast-flying, easily raised fowl are quite popular; however,

This uplander has scored on a brace of valley quail during an October hunt in eastern Washington state.

it's not, I'm told, a very accurate representation of hunting their wild brethren. Today, wild chukars are hunted throughout the Pacific Northwest – eastern Washington and Oregon, and western Idaho. The breaks above the Columbia River are a popular stomping ground for chukar chasers; however, it's the rocky crags and outcroppings that look down upon the Snake River and its famed Hells Canyon area that attract the lion's share of those who would pursue this most worthy European import.

I find the chukar a right handsome bird with his black facial stripe and eye-catching black and white bars. A grown chukar will weight a pound, give or take a couple ounces, and will be only slightly smaller than a ruffed grouse. His legs and stubby bill are both red, as is a slight ring around each eye. A white bib bordered by the black face stripe gives way to light gray underparts, a hue which continues over the back and down the tail. A dozen black and rust bars highlight each side – a most fitting accent to the chukar's wonderful wardrobe.

If you want to kill chukars, walk up, then hunt down. That's what I've always been told. Or, as some friends who make an annual pilgrimage from western Washington to the Hells Canyon country each year explain – "Get yourself an ATV, M.D. Then it's a matter of ride, park, and hunt. Ride, park, and hunt. You can cover a lot more ground that way." A challenging endeavor, chukar hunting isn't for the weak of heart nor leg. The terrain is incredibly rugged, and the birds show a passion for running uphill

Typical valley quail habitat, this in central Washington's Yakima Valley. Notice the water nearby, an important key to finding these game birds in much of the arid West.

and flushing from the very last rock at the edge of a 500-foot drop. They're strong fliers, too – even those raised by the hand of man are no slouches in the aerial performance department. Still, like the desert quail, chukars do have a weakness…they hold well after the initial covey break. Now's the time for a sharp-nosed pointing dog, one who not only can lead you to the birds, but doesn't mind the extra up-and-down associated with the retrieve.

Hungarian partridge – Huns, which also go by the name gray partridge, came, like chukars, to North America from Europe in the early part of the 20th century. Since their first introductions on the West Coast, Huns have been introduced and have proliferated – some populations more than others – across much of the western U.S. and southern Canada. Today, the Dakotas provide much of the nation's gray partridge opportunities; however, hit-and-miss hunts can be had from Iowa, Kansas, and Nebraska west to Washington and eastern Oregon.

Slightly larger than a midwestern bobwhite – perhaps 12 to 14 ounces – the Hun is a soft gray overall, save for the flanks that can show a bit of black and white streaking. Most noticeable, however, is the cinnamon or buff facial patch, a mark that begins at the bill narrowing behind the eye at the back of the head.

Native Iowan and hunting partner, Dave Fountain, explains – "Huns are creatures of habit. Where you saw that bunch at the edge of the field today…well, chances are they're going to be there tomorrow. Your best bet is to hunker down in the road ditch near that spot, and wait until they come out into the field to feed. That's the only way you're going to get close enough to jump them in range," he said. "Other than that," he continued, "you're going to need a .22-250. And even then, it's going to be a long poke." Jumpy by nature, Huns further complicate things by inhabiting relatively sparse cover; in fact, the four coveys I've seen in eastern Iowa have all been feeding in bare, chisel-plowed fields. In such cases, I'm told, a hunter's best opportunities come early in the morning and late in the evening, as the birds return to their version of heavier cover – sparse brush adjacent to barren ground – to roost. That's the time when a hunter with a close-working pointer can take advantage of these daily maneuvers. Other places, North Dakota and the Kansas grasslands, for instance, Huns are hunted much like bobwhites.

It's about the habitat

Up to this point I've tried not to project a negative, *No Pheasants Here* attitude in my dialogue. And I have to admit that at times, it's been a tough task, this staying optimistic about a wild population that in my youth I barely knew and that today, I see – well – slowly fading away in many parts of the country. No water in Nebraska and Kansas. A switch from grains to grapes in eastern Washington and California. Fields tilled and farmed within an inch of the barbed wire in Iowa. The perilous day-to-day existence of the Conservation Reserve Program (CRP), the governmental program that pays farmers to let ground set aside and produce not corn or soybeans, but vital nesting and wintering habitat...and pheasants.

But what's it all mean? First, let me preface this brief explanation with the statement that I am neither a schooled wildlife manager nor a biologist. I don't pretend to know all of the intricacies involved with each and every habitat related question; however, what I do know is this. If given a place to live, pheasants will do just that. Live. Food, water, and shelter, where shelter in terms of the ringneck can be defined as grassy nesting cover and thicker, protective wintering and loafing cover. To the best of my knowledge, it's really no more complicated than that.

And that's where Pheasants Forever (PF) comes in. Founded in 1982, PF's goal, as is put forth in their mission statement, is "*to conserve and to enhance pheasant and other wildlife populations through habitat restoration, improvements in land, water, and wildlife management policies, and public awareness and education.*" In a nutshell, this can be translated to read, as giving pheasants a place to live and letting folks know (1) that they need these places, (2) what kind of places these birds actually need, and (3) – and perhaps most importantly – how people can not only get involved, but what they can realistically do to conserve and enhance pheasant and other wild populations simply by contributing to the world around them.

"Pheasants Forever's focus is on conserving, enhancing, and increasing the quantity and quality of wildlife habitat," said Joe Duggan, vice president of development and public affairs for the Minnesota-based organization. "And in doing projects that we typically do – native grass restoration for nesting cover, wetland restoration to enhance winter cover, planting farmstead shelter belts – we're doing a couple things. In addition to specifically addressing the needs of pheasants – well, for instance. Some of the most endangered and threatened wildlife species are the neo-tropical migrants which inhabit the prairie regions of North America. They're benefiting tremendously from our work. We've done stream and riparian restoration projects in the West that have had tremendous benefits to native trout and native trout streams. The benefits to wildlife are across the board. When you stick vegetative cover on the ground where it wasn't before, you're going to provide a place for wildlife to live. And when we improve the quality and quantity of that vegetative cover we call wildlife habitat, you're making spaces for other wildlife and critters to live."

But the question remains – Is it working?

"You do see benefits. Sometimes they're immediate, and sometimes they take time. But when you install the habitat practices that we do – the nesting cover, the wetland restoration, the shelterbelts, the buffer strips – within a year or two, there is a physical difference in the landscape that you can actually see. And wildlife will move into these new areas very rapidly, and you'll start seeing pheasants and other wildlife occupying that space," said Duggan.

"Here's one of my favorite quotes on that very subject. A good friend of mine hunts South Dakota every year. He and a farmer were actually talking about the Conservation Reserve Program, and what happens if the CRP program goes away. Greg says that the farmer told him – 'Until we enrolled this ground in CRP, we didn't have pheasants around here. Not like we have today.' And Greg asked him what happens if you lose that CRP. The farmer told him – 'See that field across the road?' he asked, pointing to a field that was all plowed and under intensive agriculture. 'That's what it'll all get back to. Away will go the habitat and away will go the pheasants. You know something,' the farmer continued. 'That stuff they call habitat? That stuff really works.'"

But PF is not alone in its fight to preserve and create habitat, and educate the masses on the importance of conserving these oh-so-vital natural resources. Headquartered in Edgefield, South Carolina and founded in 1981, Quail Unlimited, Inc. mirrors PF's intensive efforts regarding grassroots, *get your hands dirty* projects designed not only to benefit the organization's namesake critter – quail – but all wildlife, game and non-game species alike. Today, QU members in more than 520 national chapters raise tens of thousands of dollars and provide information, education, and instruction to hundreds upon hundreds of concerned sportsmen and women, all of whom share a common goal – the betterment of our natural world, *regardless* of the species in the spotlight.

In the same way that NWTF efforts also benefit whitetails and Ducks Unlimited projects provide for sandhill cranes, PF and QU undertakings are helping secure the future not only for ringnecks and bobwhites, but for any of 100,000 wild, wonderful, and oh-so-irreplaceable things. These things include not only our hunting heritage, but also that of our children and their children. For more on Pheasants Forever, take a few minutes and visit their website at www.pheasantsforever.org. Or better yet, give them a call at 877-773-2070. The folks at Quail Unlimited can be reached at 803-637-5731.

Long-time Iowa trapper, Dave Fountain, prepares a double long-spring for placement on a local beaver dam.

7

The Trapper's World

The trapper's world is no bigger than the size of the pan on a Number 1 Victor leg-hold.

"He shoots. He scores! And the Mallards take the lead," said the voice on the radio. It was January, 2002. Another night in my fur shed, skinning muskrats and listening to the local hockey game on the radio. That voice from the air took me back to another winter night of the 1960s where I was again skinning muskrats and listening to a hockey game in my fur shed of that time, my grandparents' garage. Like most trappers that I know, I am connected to the past. I grew up reading about the adventures of the mountain men and their quest for beaver in the American West.

My transition to trapper started with the discovery of a bundle of rusty traps hanging on the wall of a garage at the family farm. I have been a trapper ever since. I've set traps every season after finding that bundle of traps in 1965. Some seasons, a lot of traps; some seasons, just a few. But always, traps were set.

If trapping fever bites you, trapping becomes a part of your life and who you are. A good friend of mine describes running a trapline as a little bit of Christmas morning every day as you anticipate what awaits at every set you tend.

Tom Walters is the former president of the Iowa Trappers Association, present board member, Trapper Education Instructor, and one of the last of an unfortunately dying breed.

Back on the line after 14 years away…and a buck mink on the first day!

The trappings of life

That opening line about the trapper's world? An old man told me that years and years ago, probably at a trapper's convention somewhere in central Ohio. Or maybe it was something I overhead while sitting in Jack Hatfield's fur shed, waiting for Jack to grade my small pile of muskrats, mink, and 'coon. Despite being uttered some 25 years ago, the nameless old man's words have always stayed with me.

But what significance, if any, is there to what the old man said? Well, my friend, the significance is this. The trapper looks at the world an inch at a time. He has to in order to be successful. Though I take nothing from them, trappers don't enjoy the 500-yard freedom of the modern centerfire deer hunter. Trappers don't even have the 40-yard opportunity of the turkey hunter. No, the trapper's world – his effectiveness – is only as large as the front foot of a big buck mink; or a 'coon; or a muskrat. And how is this individual able to distill infinity down to the size of a quarter? That ability, folks, is what makes trapping what it is.

Oh, there was a time when it was about the money. A time I can remember vividly, when I sold the $11 muskrats to Jack Hatfield in the late 1970s. That was when trapping and financial stability could have been considered synonymous. During this so-called heyday,

trappers, and I'll use the word *very* loosely to describe in some cases an individual who owned traps and set them outdoors in hopes of connecting with some hapless furbearer other than the neighbor's cat, were a dime a dozen. Everyone, it seemed, wanted in on the bounty.

That was the late 1970s. By 1988, those same $11 'rats had dropped to a mere 35 cents. And 'coon? When I could sell them, even the best grades brought only two to three dollars. Fact was, I was making more selling the carcasses than I was selling the hides. I won't go into that, but let's just say that there were folks out there who dearly loved raccoons… surrounded by potatoes, carrots, and celery.

The result of all this was simple and easy to explain – no money meant no trappers. Those that stayed on did so because they loved the outdoors. And they loved the challenge that trapping presented. But for 99 percent of the country's trappers, both the talented and the fly-by-nighters, the #110 conibears, #1 stop-loss, and #1.5 coil springs found their way unceremoniously into a dark, dusty corner of the garage where today, they sit quietly gathering unintentional rust and catching nothing but spider webs.

Little has changed in the 15 years since most of the nation's trappers hung up their packbaskets. Little, that is, in terms of money. The art and history that is trapping, however, has undergone a series of radical transforma-

Trapping puts an individual on a one-on-one basis with the world around him or her.

densed version of the modern history of trapping as a prelude to the how-to portion of this particular chapter for a one-word reason – encouragement. By that I mean that one of my primary goals for this chapter is to fan the flame. I know the spark is there. Those of you who have trapped in the past but have, for whatever reason or reasons, stopped, I urge you to reconsider. Unearth a half dozen #1 long-springs and a dozen #110 Conibears, knock the rust off, and set a short line on a nearby creek. And along with your equipment, make sure to take the most valuable item – someone else. It doesn't matter who – your son or daughter. A nephew. A neighbor. Someone. Show them what it is you're doing, and how. Better yet, tell them why. And for those of you who have never trapped – learn. The human resources are there, still reading issues of *Fur-Fish-Game* and *The Trapper and Predator Caller*. Get on the Internet and research your state's trapping association. Then, attend a convention. Ask questions. Sit through seminars. Follow along. I'll help, and so will hundreds of trappers, past and present, who would love nothing more than the ear of an eager student. We're willing to help pass the torch. All you have to do is accept it.

But again, I digress. What you want to read about, I'm guessing, is the science behind the art of trapping. Well, the truth is, there is no science. Trapping isn't rocket science. Oh, it can get involved, what with expensive traps, ATVs, scents, locks, dyes, and an entire alchemist's closet of concoctions and contraptions. Thing is, it *can* be intensive, but it doesn't HAVE to be. Think of it more like learning; that is, without realizing you're being schooled. Your diploma comes when you round that corner and hear that trap chain rattling. Is it a 'coon? A 'rat? Maybe a mink? Read on. We'll get there.

Muskrats

To me, muskrats are to the trapper as squirrels are to the hunter. They're a starting point. A relatively easy to come by, comfortable margin of error type of critter that can make the most inexperienced trapper feel like an E. J. Dailey, Stanley Hawbaker, or Tom Miranda. Don't get me wrong. Muskrat trapping, particularly on a large scale, is difficult, time-consuming work; still, it makes a great beginning.

Muskrats are commonly referred to simply as 'rats but are not to be confused with your basic Norway rat. They are, however, just about as widely distributed as Norway rats. Only in the most arid regions of the American Southwest and the Arctic will muskrats be absent. Today, the states of Louisiana and Mississippi are thought to be home to the country's largest population of muskrats. However, populations ranging from a handful to those of problematic proportions can be found from Washington to the Virginias and everywhere in between.

tions, most if not all having to do with a very elemental two-word phrase – politically incorrect. Fewer trappers, it seems, meant lower recruitment into the ranks. In some cases, entire generations were lost. Unexposed, they were, to the fundamentals of trapping, its educational opportunities, and its much more than valid role as a wildlife management tool. Over time, a largely uninformed and emotional general public began, however incorrectly, to compare traps and trappers to thumbscrews and the Marquis de Sade, respectively. The word trapping itself became a buzzword for archaic and barbaric. It had become politically incorrect. People thought it was wrong. Eventually, states such as Colorado, Washington, and Arizona threw the trapping issue in front of the general public. The result? Thanks to slick public relations campaigns that had more to do with emotion than fact, trapping is now prohibited in all three states. And the trapper in those states is extinct.

I digress; however, I mention this Reader's Digest con-

Ah, the prolific little muskrat, the mainstay of many a trapper's line, and often a newcomer's first catch.

I find muskrats as a rule to be relatively plain-looking creatures. They're a hump-backed little critter, with a profile much higher in the back than in the front, and not unlike that of a 1969 Chevelle sitting on oversized mag wheels and tires. Only the 'rat is brown and hairy, where the Chevy should be black with white accent striping from grill to bumper *and*, of course, have a much larger engine. But I'm off-track again.

True to its name, the muskrat does look like the more common Norway rat. It is a rich chocolate brown overall and sports an 8- to 10-inch tail, which is covered with small scales and is flattened vertically. Adults will average 1½ to 3 pounds in weight, and will measure approximately 15 to 18 inches, tail not included. Up front, the 'rat comes complete with a pair of very rodent-like, orange incisors that it uses to nip and cut foods such as cattails, roots, and grasses. Pound for pound, there are few things meaner than a cornered muskrat. This includes 'rats tethered to a short-chained #1 jump trap. Those small white scars on every veteran water trapper's hands didn't come from cutting carrots.

Muskrats are both adaptable and prolific, meaning that most environments featuring some sort of wetland area – ponds, lakes, streams, swamps, marshes, and the like –most likely harbor a population to some degree. As for being prolific, the cottontail's famed libido pales in comparison to that of the lowly but sexually lively muskrat. Muskrats have but three preoccupations – eating, hiding from mink, and breeding. Female muskrats may throw several litters each season – more in the mild climates down south, and fewer in the north – with each of these broods numbering from four to a dozen or more little ones. With numbers like that, it doesn't take long for a population to outgrow its habitat and its food sources.

'Rat sign

Muskrat sign is, with only a couple exceptions, both easy to see and relatively simple to translate. Without question the most recognizable indication of the presence of muskrats is the traditional muskrat house. These dome-shaped structures vary in size depending upon factors such as population and the availability of building materials. Houses will typically range in size from those that will fit in a large bushel basket to huge mounds the length, breadth, and height of a Volkswagen Beetle. Construction materials differ, but some of the most frequently used items include cattails, tule reeds, and small willow branches. The majority of 'rat houses will play home to multiple rodents, the number of inhabitants depending upon the size of the house and the overall population. One or more entrances or holes provide access to the security of the house's interior. Often, these holes will be literally chewed into the house at the base below the waterline; however, most huts will also feature at least one entrance/exit combination a short distance away from the house proper.

Tyler Fountain, 16, caught this 'rat at a den set on a small creek in eastern Iowa.

Speaking of dinner tables, let's talk about feedbeds. Constructed of available grasses, rushes, cattails, or similar materials and anchored often right amongst the 'rat's aquatic buffet, feedbeds are nothing more than eating platforms. These beds can range in size from that of a Frisbee to about as big around as a Hula-Hoop, and will usually be littered with pieces and parts of the 'rat's most recent meals.

No discussion on wild animals, it seems, is complete until there's a mention of droppings. And so I won't disappoint anyone, 'rat scat looks much like deer poop, only smaller, which makes a lot of sense. All kidding aside, muskrat droppings are small and oval-shaped, and can usually be found on floating logs or on mid-current rocks. Occasionally, large concentrations of droppings will be found, usually on the aforementioned log, or perhaps on what would appear to be a feedbed dedicated solely to the act of defecation. If that's what you're thinking, you're right. Muskrats, like beavers and otters, will often create regularly used toilets. It's believed that these toilets, frequently anointed as they are with droppings, urine, and scent or musk, serve both as territorial signposts and as calling cards from males to receptive females. Either way, if you find one, make sure you know where it is come opening day of trapping season 'cause it's a hot spot.

Muskrat sets that work: What you'll need, and how to do it

The traps

Let's face it. A trapper without traps is just another guy who doesn't shave, dresses funny, and gets up at all hours of the morning in order to go outside by himself and commune with nature. Give this same individual a half dozen #1 long-springs, and he becomes, at least by loose definition, a trapper.

The 'rat trapper's arsenal consists primarily of five very basic and easy-to-operate pieces of steel –

#1 long-spring – A very traditional leg-hold trap. The "#1" refers to the physical size of the trap itself. A #1 long-spring is approximately 7 inches long, with a jaw spread of 4 inches and a pan diameter of roughly 1¾ inches.

#1 jump trap – Another very traditional trap. Because there is no long spring – Get it? – the jump trap has a very low, flat profile, thus making it easy to conceal. This particular trap has a tendency to rise or "jump" upon release, allowing it to get a higher hold on the target animal. Great multi-purpose trap for 'rats, 'coon, and mink.

#1 stop-loss – Looks just like the #1 long-spring, only the stop-loss includes an auxiliary spring arm that helps hold the animal away from the trap jaws. This action

Dens not associated with houses are likewise important sign. Excellent diggers, muskrats will often burrow into streamsides, pond banks, or earthen dams. At the end of each tunnel, a chamber will be excavated and lined with cattails, bark, or grasses, and will serve as the rodent's main living quarters. In many cases, active dens are easy to see, thanks to the mud cloud caused by the animal's comings and goings; *however*, locating such den entrances can prove difficult in situations involving moving water. Here, the current carries the indicator mud away from the mouth of the den, making it necessary for the trapper to look just a little bit closer so as to visually spot the entrance. The bottom directly in front of active 'rat dens found along moving waters will frequently appear scoured or scrubbed, almost as though someone swept the front porch of the house with a whisk broom. Often, these clean areas will stand out as a light-colored portion of an otherwise dark bottom. Unlike dens, runs are nothing more than 'rat roads; the deer trails of the muskrat's world. These may be very obvious paths cut through stands of cattails or tules as a result of repeated wanderings. Or they may be as nondescript as a shallow trough snaking along a muddy bottom. Active runs are relatively easy see as they will often be muddy and will typically contain floating bits of plants and roots. Muskrats, it seems, are messy eaters, and it's this lack of manners than can help lead a trapper to a 'rat's favorite dinner table.

prevents twist-offs ('rats) and chew-outs ('coon).

#110 Conibear – One of the greatest inventions since duct tape. Also known as the killer or body-grip trap. Two steel wire squares powered by a single spring grip the 'rat fore and aft. THE ticket for setting dens and holes, and some trail applications.

#1.5 long-spring – Though some would use no other, I'll give the #1.5 long-spring an Honorable Mention in the muskrat category. Its additional weight can help make drowning sets more effective; however, for 'rats, the #1.5 can be a bit much as it fractures front leg bones on impact and facilitates twist-offs. Good 'coon trap, though.

The gear

Here, the equipment list grows a bit longer. Not complicated, mind you, just a little longer. Under most circumstances, the part-time 'rat trapper would be doing well if outfitted with the following gear –

Waders or hip boots – Self-explanatory.

Pack basket – Since you're collecting stuff, you're eventually going to need something to carry your stuff in. Enter the pack basket. Baskets today are available in traditional wood or synthetics (fiber-strips), and in sizes ranging from 13 to 30 inches deep. My suggestion is to get a size based on the length of the line you intend to run; that is, the number of traps and the amount of stuff you think you'll need. Most pack baskets come complete with shoulder straps, a great idea that leaves your hands free to do the work. No money for a basket? A five-gallon bucket, cleaned and deodorized inside, will work just fine. Whether bucket or basket, get yourself some type of belted pouch that you can attach to your container. This pouch will serve as home for scents, lures, baits, wire, wire cutters, fence staples, and any of the 1.73 million different things you'll take on the line with you.

Wire and wire cutters – With 101 uses for both, including extending chains, making drowning sets, wiring Conibears to stakes, repairing your pack basket, and on and on. I'm partial to black stovepipe wire, 11- to 14-gauge, however, specialty waxed wires are also available. As for the sidecutters, my advice is to go decent quality but as inexpensive as possible. Why? You're going to lose them before the season ends. That's why.

Hatchet – Doesn't have to be Paul Bunyan's double-bit axe, but a small hatchet in a nylon sheath will have more than its share of functions. Keep track of it, or just when you really, really need it, you'll remember you left it three sets back.

Stakes – Typically, I'll cut a supply of stakes prior to opening day, and I'll carry them into the marsh with me; however, I've also been known to cut my stakes on the spot. Either way works for me. Depends on where you're trapping and the availability of impromptu stake materials.

Conibears, or body-gripping traps as they're often called, are to the 'rat trapper what a football is to Brett Farve - an essential piece of equipment.

Scents and lures – Mink and 'coon trappers will usually place more emphasis on the use of scents and lures than will 'rat trappers. That's not to say that sweet-smelling or musky potions such as natural 'rat musk, beaver castor, anise, or oils such as peppermint or sweet flag won't attract these small rodents – they will; hence, today's market for muskrat-specific lures. For more information on this subject, I'd suggest either talking to a experienced 'rat trapper, making a phone call to your local fur dealer, or searching the Internet under the subject heading, Trapping Scents & Lures.

Zip-ties and orange marker ribbon – If you haven't found a million uses for zip-ties, also known as cable ties, by now, you're obviously not living right. Zip-ties are to the trapper what pizza and beer are to the college sophomore…a necessity. As for the ribbon, this can be used to mark your set locations; that is, if Johnny Sneak-um the Trap Thief is either absent or on vacation.

Flashlight or headlamp – Again, self-explanatory. I lean toward the headlamp as it keeps my hands free for other duties which will hopefully include pulling scores of 'rats and mink from my sets. That, or finding my sidecutters, which I just dropped in knee-deep water for the hundredth time. Good batteries. 'Nuff said.

Trapper's stick – Originally, my father used about 20 inches of an old Louisville Slugger. He cut this down,

I've used this pack basket since 1980. Good ones will last, and come in awful handy when trying to carry gear into - and fur out of - the field.

An active den in a corner of a small Iowa pond provided this November 'rat.

wrapped the handle in rawhide, and drilled the knob end for a leather thong that went around his wrist. On the business end, he installed a short stainless steel screw-hook. The hook served as a searcher and retriever of stretched trap chains and his subsequent catch; the thick portion of the Slugger was applied sharply to the base of each live 'rat or mink's skull. His original stick has since been retired, replaced by an 18-inch section of solid fiberglass sledge handle complete with a rubber-padded business end.

.22 pistol – I mention this piece here not so much for 'rats or even mink, but more for its role as a dispatcher of 'coon. Personally, I carry a light and very old German-made Buffalo Scout six-shot .22 revolver in a similarly old leather holster. Loaded with .22 shorts or CB caps, this old wheelgun makes short work of even the meanest ringtail. And the occasional fox squirrel that makes the mistake of venturing too close…and sitting still.

The Sets

How you go after these critters is based on the gear you have and the area you'll be trapping. Be flexible to be successful.

Dens and holes – With the invention of the now-familiar Conibear trap, setting muskrat holes, whether at houses or at bank dens, became as simple as tying your shoe. Just take your set #110 Conibear, place it as squarely in front of the hole as possible, and stake it securely into position. Typically, a single stake through the coil spring will suffice; however, a second stake placed through the spring arm can help stabilize the trap. Armed with a supply of traps and a matching number of pre-cut stakes, it takes but a short time to make several, perhaps dozens, of one of the most effective 'rat sets known. A couple tips are in order here though. Even though they're supposedly 'killer' traps, it's always a good idea to wire the trap ring to your stake. This prevents a trapped 'rat from thrashing itself off the stake and cuts down on the time spent searching for such runaways. Stake your Conibears as securely as possible. Again, you don't want your catch wiggling off with your steel. Conibears can be attached to small tomato-style stakes at home using wire, Zip-ties, or fence staples. It only takes seconds to push these ready-made sets into position in front of the hole or den. In places where theft isn't an issue a short ribbon of orange surveyors tape tied 'round the top of the stake aids in relocation. Believe me, even a small marsh can get awful big in a hurry when you're looking for that set you know has just got to be there…. somewhere.

Slide sets – Slides are another great bet for the 'rat trapper, and are about as easy to set as are dens. Essentially, slides are muddy, well-worn paths, typically leading from a water environment to dry ground, or vice versa. At streamside slides, a #1 long-spring or #1 jump trap is concealed at the end of the slide under approximately an inch of water; deeper (3-4 inches) if a hind foot catch is desired. No covering is necessary. Slides on houses are set in a similar fashion – 1 to 4 inches of water, no covering, staked in deeper water; however, on muskrat houses, I'll use a #1 stop-loss in place of the traditional long-spring. With so much vegetation nearby for a trapped 'rat to tangle itself in, I like the addition of the stop-loss spring as an aid in the prevention of twist-offs.

Feedbeds – Again, the #1 stop-loss or jump trap gets the nod here. 'Rats do a lot of stomping around at feedbeds, as they do on houses, so deciding where to position the trap can require a little mix of experience and luck. In the best cases, a semi-slide or slight depression on one side of the feedbed will show where the 'rat typically climbs up and on.

Mink

If memory serves me right, I was 16 or 17 the year I caught three mink in one morning. Now maybe to some that's not a big deal, but to a 16-year-old part-timer, it was like hitting the lottery and getting a "Just to say hi" phone message from Raquel Welch, all rolled into one. Nah, it was better than that, especially when you consider that all three were bucks – males – and brought me $36 each when I dropped them off at Jack Hatfield's fur shed that same afternoon. Yes, $36 was a big deal back in 1980. Or at least it was to me.

There's not a trapper alive who doesn't smile when he rounds a corner to see a tight trap chain and a #1 jump with a firm grip on the hind leg of a big buck mink. Mink are secretive little creatures, bobbing and weaving their snakelike way up and down the country's wetlands. A mink is a here today, gone tomorrow wraith that both frustrates and delights. While other furs have suffered at the marketplace, mink, despite a glut of farm-raised pelts, have also held a goodly portion of their value; still, price notwithstanding, what has never faltered where mink are concerned has been the excitement of the catch.

Description and distribution

Mink can be found all across the Lower 48, as well as all of Canada and the major portions of Alaska. Equally at home on dry land as they are in the water, mink are

Though prices are a shadow of what they once were, mink, like this fine buck here, remain a welcome addition to any day's catch.

typically associated with water of some nature. These aquatic habitats can include swamps, marshes, lakes – both large and small – and all sorts of moving waters such as streams and creeks. In fact, no setting is more traditional nor as productive as a small rocky-bottomed stream flowing through scattered Midwestern woodlots and agricultural sections.

In appearance, mink can best be described as long and skinny. Males will vary in color from brown to black, with the darker hues being more preferable from a monetary standpoint. A big buck will push the scales to 4 pounds, a little more in some places and a little less in others, and will generally measure from 18 to 20 inches in length. Add another 5 to 7 inches, give or take, for the fully furred tail, and you have a pretty impressive animal. Females are smaller, typically weighing in at around 2 pounds and stretching some 15 inches. A female will also be lighter in color, usually a soft brown and appear to be a dainty sort of beast. Don't let first impressions fool you. Mink are tremendous scrappers and highly tuned predators, with a menu that includes fish, frogs, crawdads, birds, mice... even small rabbits when available. Still, their favorite meal item remains muskrats, a note most beneficial for the trapper looking to lure passing mink to his sets.

Feeder streams are magnets to travelling mink. Here, the author sets a #1 jump in a trickle at the western end of a farmland pond.

Mink sets that work: What you'll need, and how to do it

Traps, gear, and accessories – Everything mentioned earlier – traps and gear included – will work wonderfully for mink. Personally, I've very fond of the #1 jump trap for my mink sets, again for the low profile, concealment, and the jump's high, tight hold. Some will say that where mink are concerned, the #1.5, style notwithstanding, should serve as a minimum trap size. Here I'll agree if 'coon are a constant consideration; however, it's been my experience that an animal will fight a larger, heavier trap with more determination and effort than it will a smaller unit. Maintained and in good working order, a #1 jump, long-spring, or stop-loss possesses more than enough strength and holding power for even the biggest buck mink, *without* the added fear of bone fracture. As with any trapping situation matching the equipment to the game being pursued makes for a more effective and efficient harvest.

The sets

Blind sets – These are probably the most popular, traditional, and productive mink set around; howev-er, the blind set isn't as sightless as the name might suggest. Basically, blind sets are traps placed in locations where you think a mink might at one time or another step. Let me put it this way. *If*, based on the place in question and the sign present, it looks like a mink or several mink may at one time or another place their little cat feet in that one-inch square piece of feeder stream, creek bank, or pond dam, then by all means put a #1 jump trap there. To be honest, a lot of the effectiveness of blind sets, regardless of the species in question, depends on experience. "That just looks good," the old-timer says, and in less than a week, that particular blind set has accounted for two mink, a 'rat, and a very disagreeable raccoon. Over time, this line veteran has come to know which sets will produce and those that won't. Again, it's called experience.

Pocket sets – The pocket set is easily made and can apply in many different situations. To make a pocket set, simply dig or, using your toe, kick a hole about the size of your fist – a little bigger or a little smaller isn't going to hurt anything –into the streambank. Six to 12 inches from front to back is usually plenty deep enough. If the weather and the water allow you to do this at the waterline, fantastic. In such a case, you can set your low-profile #1 jump trap ½ to 1 inch below the water's surface, and you don't have to concern yourself with bedding and covering the trap. For dry land sets, a shallow and stable – you don't want the trap to rock back and forth should the mink step on one of the jaws or the frame before he steps on the pan – bedding and a light covering of nearby native material will be in order. When covering most sets, the key words are "carefully" and "light." Too much cover can actually prevent a trap's jaws from closing completely, as can small sticks, pebbles, or other hard materials.

To finish the pocket set, bait and lure are secreted in the rear of the hole. What kind of bait? A quarter-sized dollop of any one of the many commercially prepared mink baits would be a good place to start; however, I've had my best luck using either the meaty hind leg of a muskrat or, better yet, a whole English sparrow. If using sparrows, strip a few feathers from the bird before tucking it into the rear of the hole. Scattering these around the entrance adds to the visual effectiveness of the set. Finally, three or four drops of gland lure sprinkled on a cotton ball and tossed into the dark recesses of the pocket complete the set.

A FINAL NOTE – Though some of the old-school trappers might scoff at the notion, Conibears were made for mink and mink trappers. The very popular #110 works well, as does the #120. The #220 is a bit on the big side for mink; however, we'll discuss that in the next chapter on 'coon. The list of Conibear possibilities for the mink trapper is virtually endless. Guarding a pocket set; as a blind set between two rocks or at a pinch point in a creek;

a trail set; or armed in front of an old muskrat hole which has been laced with a part of its former owner – they're all excellent sets.

Raccoon

Familiar to most, the raccoon makes his home in every state in the Lower 48. His numbers will be lowest in the mountainous West and the arid regions of the American Southwest; still, everyone everywhere, including those residing in parts of Alaska and southern Canada, has a pretty good chance of running into a 'coon or two.

Despite the existence of more than a dozen different subspecies, there's really no way to mistake a raccoon for anything else. First, there's the black mask. Then there's the ringed tail. Between the two, there's a gray, fuzzy, generally pudgy appearance. And finally, there's the dead giveaway: If it's getting into something, some sort of mischief such as rooting through your garbage cans or turning your chimney into a mammalian maternity ward – well then, it's a raccoon. Almost guaranteed.

There are some differences, though. Southern 'coon, for instance, will run a little smaller and will appear a little skinnier. Fur volume – who needs a fur coat in Mississippi? – plays a role here; however, those animals living below the Mason-Dixon Line are just going to be a bit smaller than, say, 'coon living in the Upper Midwest or the New England states. The best 'coon in the country, that is the heaviest and most well-furred, come from the northern states of Michigan, Wisconsin, and Minnesota, as well as Maine, Vermont, New Hampshire, and southern Canada. That's not to say that you won't find excellent 'coon in states such as the Dakotas, Iowa, Ohio, New York, and Pennsylvania, only that the buyers for the most part are partial to what they refer to as 'Northern 'Coon.'

'Coon sets that work: What you'll need, and how to do it

Traps, gear, and accessories – As far as 'coon traps are concerned, there's a couple schools of thought here. The first says that due to the 'coon's strength and ferocity when captured, anything less than a #1.5 coilspring is far too small. Better yet, a #2, either a double long-spring or a double coil. The second group, quite opposite the first, claims that a good, strong long-spring or jump, Size #1, is more than adequate. A trapped 'coon, they say, won't fight a smaller trap as it will a larger, heavier piece. Personally, my largest 'coon to date, a 24-pound Ohio female, was caught and held fast *by a toe* in an old Victor long-spring. Size? Zero. That's right, #0.

Conibears, whether set in 'rat dens, pinch points, or travel routes such as this small culvert pipe, are excellent locations for mink...and the mink trapper.

A #1.5 coil-spring. Strong, small, lightweight, and easily concealed, this piece of steel was tailor-made for the 'coon trapper.

Preparing to set a #220 Conibear in a heavily used woodland trail. These big 'bears are fine 'coon traps; however, care needs be paramount in their use.

Here, the author places a #1.5 coil-spring in front of a pocket set along a well-used trail. This trap was full the next morning.

What I should add at this point is the fact that at the time, I was 10 and didn't have much of a clue. Apparently the big old female 'coon didn't have a clue either. Or she would have simply shaken that little trap off like just another mosquito bite and walked on down the creek. Luck, it seems, plays a role in a little bit of everything. If you're looking for a happy medium between the two schools of trap thought, I might recommend the #1 double coil spring; in fact, I'd highly suggest it. True, they're a bit more expensive than your basic #1 long-spring or non-coil jump, but not so much as your larger #2. What's more, they're small, flat, and strong – exactly what you're looking for in a good 'coon trap.

The Sets

Cubby sets – There are several nice things about cubby sets for 'coon, a *cubby* being a small enclosure, usually fashioned from natural materials such as logs or rocks. They're easy to make, and can be made far in advance of the season, thus saving you time once opening day rolls around. Secondly, cubbies are a natural attractant. There's not a 'coon on the planet that can pass up a little slice of darkness that comes complete with a *Pssssst! Buddy! Over here!* kind of smell spilling forth. Third, cubbies are simple to set. Just leave an opening in your little house, put a little commercial 'coon bait and lure in the

Sharpening up the steel prior to an evening spent skinning in front of the woodburner. It really doesn't get any better that this.

'coon bait, a locked and loaded #220 Conibear. My first concern was for the two labs, both of whom had likewise discovered the great-smelling buckets. Fortunately, neither of them got a steel slap on the snout; however, each got a smack on the butt and a *BAD DOG!*, lessons which surprisingly enough, they have remembered ever since.

But a #220 in a bucket? Seems it's a very traditional 'coon set in The Hawkeye State, as it is elsewhere in the Midwest; that is, except in my native state of Ohio, where trappers are required by law to completely submerge any Conibear or body-gripping trap larger than #110. I guess that's why it caught me so off-guard to see something like this. Investigating further, which basically means asking around, I learned that most Iowa 'coon trappers will at one time or another run a line consisting primarily of buckets and #220s. Why? They're simple, quick, and deadly effective.

The trapper's other targets

I do want to mention some of the other furbearers that capture the attention of our nation's trappers. Fascinating critters such as –

Marten and fishers – Relatives of the mink, though larger, both marten and fishers are found in Canada and portions of Alaska; however, fishers, though uncommon, do reside in the New England states and were reintroduced in Wisconsin a few years back, while marten can occasionally be found in the American West.

Coyotes – Chances are there's at least one coyote within a mile of where you're sitting right now. After all, there are coyotes living in New York's Central Park. Though primarily sought by riflemen, coyotes are still trapped using conventional methods, particularly in parts of the West and Southwest.

Fox – Both species are relatively well distributed across the United States; however, as a rule of thumb – Reds seem to thrive in more open terrain, like that found in the agricultural Midwest, whereas the more secretive gray fox is very much at home in the brush, tangles, and hills commonly associated with other portions of the country.

Nutria – Introduced to the southern U.S. around 1900 as a source of fur, the nutria has since made itself at home in most of Louisiana and Mississippi's wetland areas, and can today be found as far away as Washington state and Michigan. Basically, nutria look like big muskrats – huge orange incisors, funny feet, brown fur,

back, and guard the front door with an appropriately-sized piece of steel. And let's not forget the soon to be mentioned #220 Conibear. I can't begin to tell you how many 'coon have fallen to a #220 positioned in front of a stone cubby. The numbers, I'm sure, are staggering.

Bucket sets – Upon moving to Iowa in 1997, I was accidentally introduced to an alternative to the traditional natural cubby set for raccoon. Pheasant hunting on a nearby farm during mid-November, I noticed what looked like several surveyor's stakes. The odd thing was their location, which was along a creek right at what people in the geography business would call The Middle of Nowhere. Looking back, I should have known instantly what they were. But I didn't. Suddenly, I noticed my wife's black lab, Jet, investigating something at the base of one of the stakes. And it hit me – TRAPS! Sure enough, a local trapper had made a number of mink and 'coon sets both on and just off the water, including several which consisted of a white plastic 5-gallon bucket. A closer look revealed that the buckets had been notched at opposite points along the rim and contained, in addition to a can of sardines or an unidentifiable blob of what I assumed was

The fur shed is not nearly as common a sight as it once was - unfortunately.

and a generally bad disposition. The one major difference is a round tail.

Beaver – Without question the greatest construction worker on the face of the planet. Like their smaller cousin, the muskrat, beavers can be found throughout much of the Lower 48, Canada, and Alaska, the only exception being the arid American Southwest. At one time nearly extirpated across much of its original range by unregulated trapping, beaver populations today are strong and growing, and the animal represents one of the nation's true wildlife management success stories. Oh, yeah – big, brown, flat tail, and webbed hind feet. Builds dams, cuts down trees, and lives in a house made of sticks and mud called a lodge.

Otters – Today, otter trapping is a thing primarily of the southern U.S and the mountainous West. Most states – Iowa, Missouri, and Ohio, for example – currently have on-going otter reintroduction programs in place designed to begin and build wild populations of these incredible animals.

Bobcats and lynx – In the Lower 48, bobcats inhabit the eastern and western thirds of the country, as well as much of the South and Southwest. Only in the Midwest are these secretive little cats rare; however, sightings of bobcats in states such as Iowa, Illinois, and Indiana

are growing more and more frequent each year. Lynx, on the other hand, are confined primarily to portions of Canada and Alaska, with a small population of animals living in the still-wild regions of the Pacific Northwest.

Weasels – Trappers in North America can choose from three different species – the short-tailed (West and Northwest); the long-tailed (Damn-near nationwide); and the Least (Canada and the northern U.S.). All look like a mink in miniature; however, the short-tailed is the only one that turns completely white in the winter.

Skunks and opossums – Though found almost everywhere, opossums are most common in the Midwest, East, and Southeast. Skunks come in a couple varieties – the ubiquitous striped version, and the spotted, which makes its home in the South and West. The common denominator? Both stink.

This chapter has been but an overview of trapping designed to whet the appetite of those who might someday decide to help manage animal populations in this way. Trapping is a great way to introduce kids to the outdoors and encourage responsible stewardship. It's something to think about, and more importantly something to try.

We never field-dressed our squirrels. Some folks do. It's your decision, and there is no wrong answer.

8

From field to feast

The first wild game I cleaned by myself was a fox squirrel. Come to think of it, the second wild game animal I cleaned, again by myself, was a fox squirrel. And the third. And fourth. And for the next two years, or until I reached the ripe old age of 10 and climbed the evolutionary ladder to the rung of duck shootist, I cleaned squirrels. Lots and lots of squirrels.

This was 1972, and I'd just entered the ranks of hunters. And as such, I was immediately introduced via my father to the responsibilities that come once the hunt was over – game cleaning. At the time, my father, now retired, was teaching biology at a small high school in northeastern Ohio. I say this for two reasons. The first actually deals not with my father, but with his younger brother, Jim. Seems Jim never learned, while growing up on the farm and helping to stock the larders with cottontails, how to clean rabbits, a fact which he was quick to remind folks of when it came time to process the day's bag. Oh, he was a tremendous shooter, both with a shotgun and a .22 rimfire; but cleaning – well, that was another matter altogether. So, Jim's apparent lack of knowledge, combined with the fact that my Dzedo, my Slovak grandfather, wasn't about to clean rabbits when he had a pair of strapping young sons to do such work, left but one solution – my Pop. So Pop cleaned a ton of rabbits; that is, when he wasn't beating up his younger brother.

Apparently afraid that I, too, might never learn to clean game, my Pop turned to his biology background in order to make game cleaning less of a task and more, well, interesting. "Let's see what this one's been eating," he'd say as he nicked the fox squirrel's stomach and held it up to his nose for an olfactory examination. "Just as I thought. Beech. They're always in beech this time of year." Sometimes the result of his cleaning table surgery was oak. "Indians used to make pancakes out of acorns. Acorns are bitter things, but they would wash and rinse them in water to get rid of some of that bitterness before making pancakes. Bread, too."

Truth of the matter is, Pop's impromptu biology and natural history lessons, though fascinating and greatly appreciated, weren't really necessary. For me, cleaning a rabbit or big, fat fox squirrel, plucking a cockbird, or skinning and stretching a muskrat offered not only an interesting challenge, but was a part of the whole that was the outdoor experience. What's more, I viewed the process – and still do today – as my responsibility as both a consumptive user and well-rounded outdoorsman. I welcome the opportunity that game preparation affords me to learn more about my quarry. And, last but certainly not least, I thoroughly enjoy the smell and taste of a Dutch oven filled with a bubbling mixture of cottontail rabbit, mushrooms, tomatoes, and a sweet Georgia vadalia onion. So if nothing else, I like to eat; therefore, I must clean game.

Good eats start in the field

Wild game will taste either good or not-so-good for several reasons. Among these qualifiers are the type of game taken, its age, the manner in which it was killed – lung shot versus paunch shot, for example – and its diet at the time it was harvested; however, there is one variable that, regardless of those already mentioned, will *always* influence the end result. How was the game handled in the field?

Let's take a look at several different species and how they might best be tended to both in the field and in transit from the field to your game cleaning station.

Squirrels – My Pop never field-dressed his squirrels. I don't either; however, some folks do, saying that it's best to get the entrails out to lessen the chance of

Birds, like these Nebraska grouse, can be drawn (gutted) in the field, particularly if the temperatures are warm.

the contents of perforated innards contaminating the meat, and to speed the cooling process. I opt for the non-field-dressing route for two reasons. One, I use a .22 rim-fire for almost all of my squirrel hunting, and therefore – hopefully – don't have to concern myself with multiple pellets puncturing stomachs and intestines. And two, I see field-dressing squirrels as a great opportunity to transfer millions of hairs from the hide to my soon-to-be lunch. Instead, and particularly during the early part of the season when temperatures can be quite high, I'll carry my bushytails either by hand or on a game strap from place to place and lay them in the shade at each new location. What I **won't** do is pile them up in a non-breathable game bag or pouch where heat can collect, and the fleas and ticks which are departing their former host have easy access to their next meal – me. Once at the truck, I'll lay the squirrels in a cooler with a couple sections of yesterday's newspaper separating the animals from the bag of ice in the bottom. Later in the season as temperatures fall, I'll skip the cooler and ice step.

Rabbits
– My Pop *always* field-dressed his rabbits. I do too. Are you starting to see a pattern here? Anyway, field-dressing your bunnies accomplishes two things. First, it lessens the weight you have to carry in your game bag. And, secondly, it helps start the cooling process. Yes, field-dressing your cottontails does increase that chances that you'll wind up with a handful of tiny

gray and brown hairs on the carcass, so I'll let you decide. As for transporting rabbits in the field, I've always gone the back-of-the-hunting coat route. Rabbit season, at least in the northern portions of the country, typically comes complete with mild to downright chilly temperatures; readings that accelerate heat dissipation and cause me little if any concern should I have three or four bunnies in the game bag.

Upland game birds
– This includes pheasants, quail, grouse, and the like. I don't field-dress the upland birds that I harvest. I just don't see any reason to; that is, unless the temperatures are extremely warm for that time of year. Should that be the case, then, yes, I have been known to very quickly and simply draw – gut – my birds, again, merely to speed the cooling process.

Doves
– I'm putting doves in a category of their own simply because doves and hot weather are relatively synonymous terms. Part of our regular dove hunting equipment is a soft-sided camouflage cooler. Inside the cooler is a small bag of ice, several plastic bottles of water, and a couple sections of newspaper. The ice keeps the water, which we drink, cold. The ice also helps cool our doves, which are laid on a section of newspaper over the bag of ice. It's all lightweight, compact, and easily carried. Unfortunately, I still need a small U-Haul truck to transport enough ammunition for a 15-dove limit.

Squirrels are anything but difficult to clean, IF you remember a couple things - sharp knife, and water.

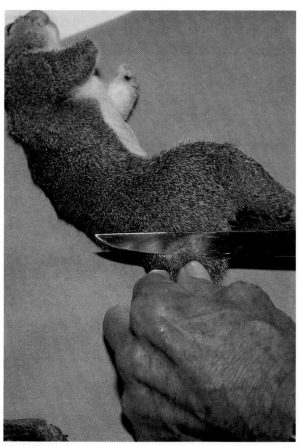

The tail goes...

Step by step – Squirrels and rabbits

Among the many things my father taught me is that there is a one-word secret to skinning squirrels and rabbits *without* getting fur on the meat. And that one word is water.

Seems years ago, while my father was attending college at Ohio University in Athens, he was known to spend quite a few evenings at the Waterloo Wildlife Experimental Station west of town. In fact, he was squirrel hunting on the very evening he was to have his first date with the lady who in 1963 would become Mrs. Michael E. Johnson. He was late for their date, not leaving the woods until the last gray squirrel had crawled into its den tree; she, however, was understanding, and the rest, as they say, is history. Today when he leaves with gun in hand, she just looks and says, "Whatever." But I digress...

Apparently, it was the field staff at Waterloo who revealed to my father the secret of hairless squirrels. "Run 'em under water. Get 'em soaking wet BEFORE you start to skin them," they told him. I'm going to guess that this instruction was given in 1960. Maybe 1961. Now, some 41 years later, my Old Man still soaks his squirrels as Step One in the skinning process. "Why change what works," he says, running another big fox squirrel under the faucet. Can't argue with that one, Pop.

Today, I know folks who don't squirrel hunt simply because they either don't know how to skin the little crit-

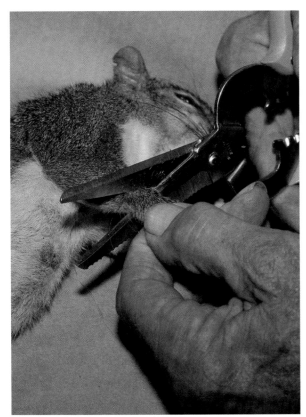

Game shears - or tin snips, or a sharp knife - are then used to remove all four feet.

Once he's soaking wet, pinch a fold of skin on the back and make your cut.

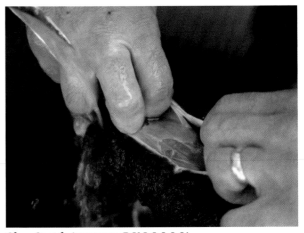

Okay, Stretch Armstrong. P-U-L-L-L-L-L!

ters, or they have become so frustrated with trying to separate squirrel from skin – often ending up with what frighteningly resembles a hairy ballpark frank– that they've given up the game. It's a shame because the truth is, it's really not all that difficult *if* you remember the water.

Step 1 – With a sharp, heavy-bladed knife, remove the squirrel's head at the neck and the tail close to the body.

Step 2 – Remove all four feet at the first joint. After years of using a knife for this step, I've since gone to a medium-heavy, but short handled pair of tin snips for this foot-removal stage. Game shears work well too.

Step 3 – Now, soak the squirrel thoroughly under running water. Keep the water running, as it's an important part of the remainder of the process.

Step 4 – Next, take a pinch of hide on the back of the squirrel directly above the spine between your thumb and forefinger – Right or left hand, whichever you're most comfortable with – and using the same sharp blade as in Step 1, make a small (1") slice through the hide. Be careful not to score the flesh itself. Rinse the knife blade to remove any hair so as not to transfer that hair

in subsequent steps. Here, I transfer the squirrel between my right and left hands as I rinse the free hand before proceeding.

Step 5 – Place your first and second fingers of each hand into the cut you've made, and P-U-L-L-L-L-L in opposite directions. On a young squirrel, each half of the hide should pop right off, inside out, just like a glove. Older squirrels, however, may require a bit more pulling, as well as a change of hands. Remember to rinse your hands during the process so as not to get hair onto the meat. Often, these same older animals may call for a bit of knifework on that narrow strip of belly hide that inevitably stays connected as you work the skin in their opposite directions. Once the hide's been removed, rinse the carcass. You're almost there.

TIP – Every skinless squirrel will have a small clump of hairs, only six or eight strands, attached to a tiny pedicle of flesh, one on each front leg right at the wrist. A second or two of knife work, and these can be easily removed. Don't forget them. My father will remind you.

Step 6 – Laying the now nude squirrel on its back, take the tip of your knife and insert it at the top of what would be the animal's pelvis, or where you would imagine the animal's pelvis and spine to meet. Run the tip through to the cutting board, and then carefully bring the blade down through the pelvis, essentially cutting the back portion into two halves.

Step 7 – Lay the squirrel in your left hand – Right-handers…lefties do the opposite. With the knife held blade up, insert the tip into the cut you've just made. Carefully, and without puncturing the internal organs, run the blade toward the head – Or where the head used to be! Once you encounter the rib cage, push the blade firmly until the tip shows through the neck opening. Now lift your knife hand, and the blade should slice cleanly through the rib cage, thus exposing the whole of the body cavity.

Step 8 – Every squirrel hunter has his or her own way of removing the animal's innards. Me, I grab the squirrel's windpipe and esophagus with my thumb and forefinger, and, using my remaining three fingers as a sort of improvised scoop, work from head to tail. With a little practice, you'll be able to remove all the entrails in one motion and in one piece. TIP – Bending the hips until they disjoint allows for a complete cleaning of the lower portion. Rinse well, and what you're left with is a completely hairless squirrel.

A FINAL NOTE – Some folks are adamant about removing the small scent glands, sometimes referred to as kernels, which are located under each forelimb in what would be the armpit region. Typically, these will be slightly smaller than a small pea, and will be light tan in color. I personally don't worry about them, but it's said that they can impart a poor taste to the meat if left in. It's your call. And finally, you'll want to cut free that small section of white connective tissue – It looks like a milky white flap of skin – which joins each hind leg with the animal's side.

And so goes squirrel cleaning from start to finish. Rabbits, by the way, can be very easily done using the exact same steps. The only difference with rabbits being that where squirrel hide can be compared to leather, rabbit skin ranks right up there with wet Kleenex. With rabbits, constantly running your hands, your knife, and the

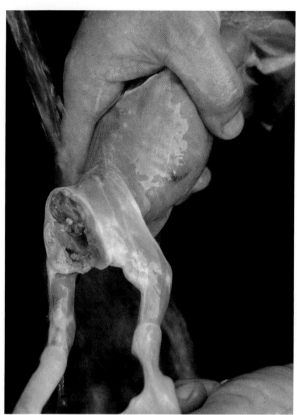

Peel the skin off like a glove. Don't forget the small hairs! Then remove the entrails, rinse, and the task is complete.

bunny under running water as you pull and remove the hide is the secret. Everything else is the same.

Step by step – Upland game birds

I'm going to divide the section titled *Upland Game Birds* into two categories: large birds, which will include pheasants, grouse, quail, prairie chickens, and similarly sized fowl – I know, they're not very big, but it's my book. And small birds, including snipe, rails, and doves. I make this distinction primarily because the methods I'm about to use for the preparation of the larger game birds can be used on the smaller; however, the opposite, as you'll soon see, is not always true. That said, onto *Larger Birds* –

Dry-plucking

Of the cleaning methods available, dry-plucking is my favorite. It's easy, time efficient, and does not eliminate one of my best-loved parts of any wild game bird, the skin. The downside, if there is one, to dry-plucking also involves this skin. Many game birds, with pheasants, grouse, and quail providing excellent examples, have a relatively thin skin that is easily torn. This is particularly true around those areas of the bird at which the hide has already been damaged, such as around shot holes or – Heaven forbid – canine tooth marks. Often, the mere act

Plucking gamebirds like this rooster pheasant is easy, quick, and makes for a wonderful presentation on the table.

of dry-plucking is enough to further tear the skin causing, at least to me, consternation and an immediate progression to yet another form of game processing – skinning.

However, it's dry-plucking we're addressing here.

Step 1 – Hold the bird in your left hand (right for you lefties), head away from you. Using your thumb and forefinger, grasp small clumps of feathers and pull *against* the grain. Continue on the breast, sides, underwings, and back. Be particularly careful around any shot-torn sections, as well as on the thin skin of the upper breast and neck areas. For now, there's no need to concern yourself with the many small hair-like feathers. We'll address those later.

Step 2 – With the bird completely plucked, remove the head, leaving as large a portion of the neck as you wish. The tail can be removed just ahead of the vent (anal opening) by cutting through the backbone. Doing so not only removes the tail and the vent proper, but also the oil glands located near the base of the tail.

Step 3 – The wings provide two options. Some folks – I'm not one of them – will take the time to fully pluck the wings. Yes, there is a bit of meat available on each wing, and, yes, the

final roasted result does make for a more eye-catching presentation; however, the process is somewhat time-consuming. As with many things outdoors, the choice is ultimately yours. The second, and more popular, option is simply to remove the wings. A cut in the "armpit" region of the wing, and the entire appendage can be easily popped out of joint. Cutting through the tendon connecting the ball to the socket completes the task.

Step 4 – Now for those small hair-like feathers. Sure, you can take the time to pluck each individual feather, one by one. Or you can do like we do, and get yourself a propane torch. Light the fire, crank the controls down so that you're working with a relatively low blue flame, and, holding the bird by the legs which you *have not* cut off yet, give it the once-over. Any feathers or down will instantly be singed away. You're not trying to George Foreman this rooster with a blowtorch. A quick sweep over the bird is usually enough to take care of most, if not all, of the light feathers, down, or pinfeathers. *Don't* try to singe your birds with an improvised torch made of rolled-up newspaper. One, you will burn yourself...it's part of the process. And

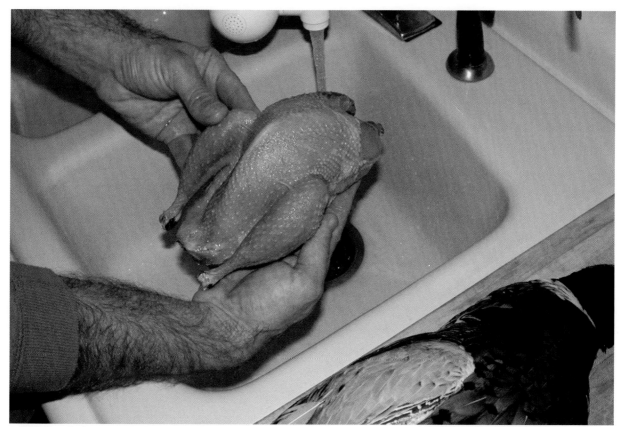

A 'before' and 'after.' Dry-plucking is probably the simplest method for handling gamebirds, though there are other ways.

secondly, the inks used in the newspaper, once set aflame, can impart a rather poor taste to an otherwise excellent meal.

Step 4 – All that remains are the entrails. Here, I'll make a small incision starting at the point where the vent had been and continuing three or four inches to either the left or the right of the 'V' which is the bottom of the breast. Through this incision, I'll remove all of the innards, taking care not to forget the lungs. These pinkish-red sponge-like organs are found on either side of the backbone. Turning the bird around, pull the crop from the neck area – more precisely, where the 'arms' of the wishbone come together – and except for a quick rinse, your task is complete….almost

Step 5 – The legs. Like the wings, there are a couple choices here. If you're big on implements such as small game cleaning shears, a quick snip right above the knee – Do pheasants have knees? – joint, and the feet vanish; however, why splinter bone like that? A better alternative is simply to cut the feet off…but where to cut? Think of it like this. Make two fists, and then put your fists together with your knuckles touching. These fists are the upper and lower joints on the bird's

leg. Connecting your fists are strong tendons and ligaments. Cutting these tendons separates the two joints. With this in mind, take the bird's foot in your left hand, knife in your right. Use the full weight of the bird to bend or open the joint. Cut across the joint where the 'knuckles' come together. The bird's weight will further pull the joint apart. Another small cut or two, and it's time for the other leg.

Step 6 – And finally, the innards. These include the gizzard, the heart, and the liver. All can be cleaned and rinsed, and either eaten by themselves or used in such things as soup stock, dressing, or gravy. Hearts and livers require little cleaning; just a quick rinse. Gizzards, muscular grinding organs that they are, must be split almost in half, and the grit and lining removed before rinsing.

Wet-plucking, or scalding

At the risk of sounding far too elemental here, there is but one difference between the dry-plucking and scalding methods of game bird processing. One uses water; the other does not. It's just that simple.

Scalding, or dipping your birds in extremely hot water prior to plucking, is favored by some who say that the

125

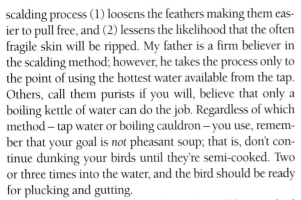

Skinning is quick, yes, but it does remove that moisture barrier. And besides, the skin tastes good.

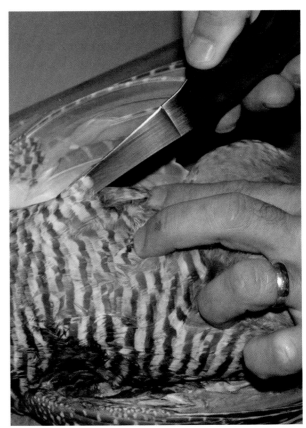

The first step is to cut through the skin - only - of the breast.

scalding process (1) loosens the feathers making them easier to pull free, and (2) lessens the likelihood that the often fragile skin will be ripped. My father is a firm believer in the scalding method; however, he takes the process only to the point of using the hottest water available from the tap. Others, call them purists if you will, believe that only a boiling kettle of water can do the job. Regardless of which method – tap water or boiling cauldron – you use, remember that your goal is *not* pheasant soup; that is, don't continue dunking your birds until they're semi-cooked. Two or three times into the water, and the bird should be ready for plucking and gutting.

As is the case with most things, the scalding method has both its pros and cons. On the plus side, scalding does appear to accomplish the aforementioned pair of objectives – easier plucking, and less tearing of skin. However, there is the mess involved with the wet, soggy feathers. There's also the need for very hot water or a way to heat three to four gallons of water to darn near boiling. Third – but who's counting? – you'll need a container into which to dip your bird. And finally, there's the smell. Ever smell a poultry operation after a good rain? Take it from me; it's not Paul Sebastin. Or even Old Spice, for that matter.

Skinning

Here, let me cut straight to the chase and get to the pros and cons of skinning. With a little bit of experience,

skinning upland game birds is quick and easy. It will also leave you with a nice-looking end product. There's no water to boil and no stinky wet chicken smell; *however*, skinning does eliminate one of my favorite parts of any wild game bird, the skin, which not only tastes good, but also serves as a ready-made roasting bag during the cooking process.

Still, if skin you must, it's a quite simple process. For this verbal demonstration, I'll use a nice rooster pheasant; however, the same steps can be applied regardless of the species.

Step 1 – With a sharp knife, cut through the skin – and ONLY the skin – along the keel (center) of the breastbone roughly from the neck to the vent. A flexible fillet knife is perfect for this surgical portion of the process.

Step 2 – Next, pull the skin away from each half of the breast, working in opposite directions. Continue, slowly and carefully, separating skin from flesh on the sides and along the upper portion of the breast. Below the breast, skin only to the vent.

Step 3 – Carefully slide the skin down the leg or drumstick to the first joint. Using your knife, cut through the joint and remove the scaled por-

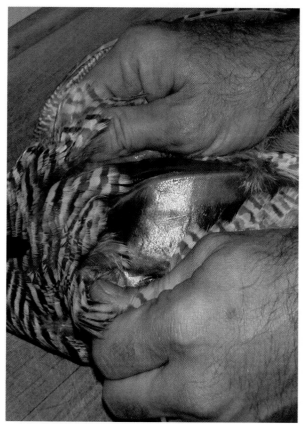

Peeling the skin away exposes the breast.

The legs are skinned, and the scaled feet removed.

tion of the leg and foot. Repeat on the other leg. Done correctly, the feet and scaled leg portions will remain on the skin.

Step 4 – Again, carefully, cut through the bird slightly ahead of the vent. The trick here is to cut through the backbone and flesh, but *not* through the skin on the opposite side. You'll see just why in a moment. As for the hole you've just created, this will be used to access the body cavity.

Step 5 – Using the tail section as a handle, you can now skin the back. Continue to a point just behind the wings. Always be careful on the back as the skin is typically very thin and easily torn. Remove or disjoint the wings using Step 3 as detailed in the Dry-Plucking section above. Like the feet, the wings should stay attached to the skin.

Step 6 – Finally, the whole of the skin – wings, feet, and tail – can be pulled toward the head, skinning the neck to a point of your choosing. A little knife work, and the bird's now skinless. Now all that's left are the entrails and a little rinse.

Filleting

I have to admit that I very seldom fillet my upland game birds. Ducks and geese, yes, but upland birds – no; however, there are still those out there who would fillet. And for them, I include the following steps.

Step 1 – Split the skin, and *just* the skin, from stem to stern. In other words, with the bird – we'll use a rooster pheasant for our verbal demonstration purposes here – on its back, make a cut through the skin only along the keel (the raised portion of the breastbone that separates the two halves) of the breast from the throat to the vent.

Step 2 – Pull the skin, feathers and all, aside from each half of the breast.

Step 3 – With the whole of the breast now exposed, insert the tip of your knife – a flexible fillet knife works very well – on one side or the other at the point where the keel connects to the 'V-shaped' clavicle or wishbone. Push the tip into the breast until resistance is felt. This is the breastplate. Now, with the tip of the knife against the breastplate *and* the side of the knife firmly against the keel, draw the blade toward the vent. Repeat on the opposite side.

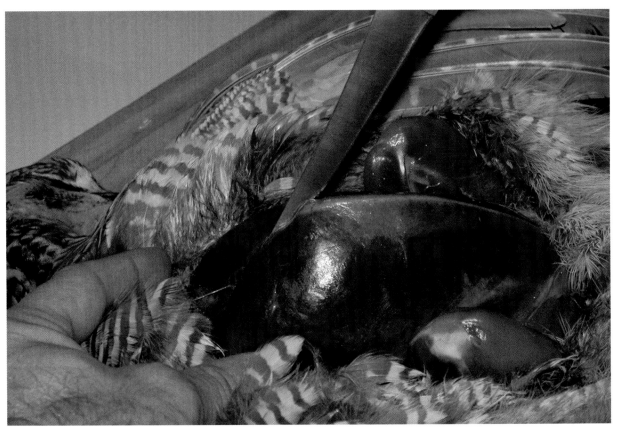

For filleting, a flexible blade (7-9 inches) knife works very well.

Step 4 – Reinsert your knife at the starting point with the blade *away* from you. This time, run the blade toward the head and against one side of the wishbone. Again, repeat on the other side.

Step 5 – Taking the fillet in your off (non-knife wielding) hand, place the blade in one of the cuts made along the keel. Once you hit the breastplate, turn the handle either right or left, depending on which side you started on, and carefully trim the fillet away from the plate. Continue working the fillet free to the side and to the front. Finally, cut the fillet away from the area around the wing joints, and you're finished.

The little ones – Doves, quail, etc.

Personally, I'll handle those birds that I place in the "small" category in either one of two ways – plucking, or breasting. Often, I'll pluck these small fowl simply because I like the way they look when served whole.

Step 1 – Please refer to Steps 1 through 6 under *Plucking* above. Same steps, smaller bird. .

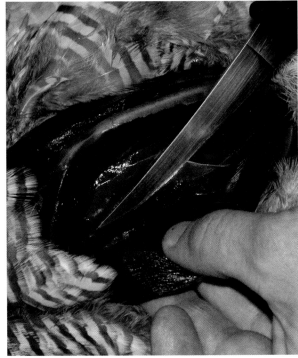

Fillet one side away, and then the other. Filleting is quick; however, some folks contend that there's quite a bit of waste involved in this method.

Plucking doves. The small gamebirds are a breeze to clean in any number of different ways.

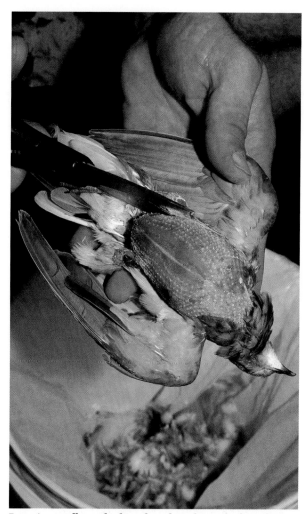
Breasting small gamebirds such as doves begins by first plucking the breast, and then trimming the breast away using snips or game shears.

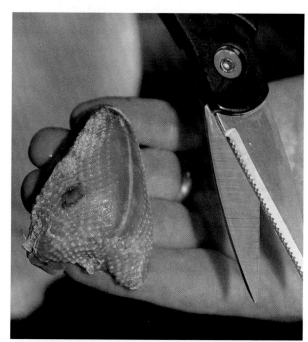
The finished product, ready for a rinse, a roll in seasoned flour, and a quick fry in bacon grease.

Breasting these smaller fowl is a bit different. Not complicated, mind you, just different –

Step 1 – Holding the dove, on its back in your right hand, place your left palm on the bird's breast.

Step 2 – Next, push your left thumb through the thin belly wall between the point (end) of the breast and the vent.

Step 3 – While maintaining a firm grip on the bird, squeeze the breast tight between your fingers and thumb, and lift up sharply. It does take a little practice, but just think of it as peeling an orange. The breast should pull free of the ribs and be attached only at the wings and two points on the collarbone (wishbone).

Step 4 – Using your game shears, snip the wings free at the body joint and the wishbone at its points of attachment. Now, place your thumb under the upper-most (fattest) part of the

These are actually snipe; however, doves done whole can be floured and pan-fried with onions just the same.

breast, and pull the breast away from the feathered skin.

Step 5 – Often, the heart will remain inside the breast. Remove this, rinse, and reach for the next bird. It's just that simple.

Recipes

In his wonderful work, *Grouse & Woodcock: A Gunner's Guide*, Don Johnson says matter-of-factly – "Since this is not a cookbook, I am going to refrain from describing preparations at great length."

I, too, feel the same about this project; that is, I see the in-the-field instruction and the story-telling as holding a higher place than would any collection of recipes and what-nots. HOWEVER, I simply can't let you folks get away without relating at least a handful of some of the finest albeit the simplest small game and upland bird recipes that I've had the pleasure to create, re-create, or merely enjoy.

My Father's Rabbit

I'd love to be able to present the history behind the recipe I'll call *My Father's Rabbit*, but unfortunately, (1) I don't know what it is, and (2) the folks weren't home when I tried to call to ask about it. On a good note, the history behind the recipe is really neither here nor there. What is important is that this particular conglomeration is as simple as it is good. Read on –

Wash, rinse, and pat dry two rabbits. That's 10 pieces (four front legs, four back legs, and two backs). Dip each piece in a bowl of mixed egg and milk, and drop each piece in a Ziplock containing flour seasoned with salt, ground pepper, and a little garlic powder. Knock off the excess flour, and brown the pieces in a little olive or canola oil. Drain on a couple sheets of paper towel.

Now, take yourself an old-fashioned Dutch oven. In the bottom, place a layer of stewed (canned) tomatoes. Then a handful of sautéed or canned mushrooms, a few pieces of broccoli, and several slices of sweet Vidalia or

Walla Walla onion. Next goes a layer of browned rabbit pieces. Then more tomatoes, mushrooms, broccoli, and onion…AND, and this is important, a couple 5- or 6-inch pieces of hot Italian sausage. It's key to the success of this recipe so don't forget them. Continue layering until the rabbit has been used. Slap the cover on that Dutch oven, and slide it into a 375-degree oven for 1.5 hours. Serve over plain white rice. It's awesome! And what's more, leave it in the Dutch oven in the 'fridge for storage because it's one of those left-over dishes like chili or spaghetti that only gets better with age.

Grouse in the fire

Julie introduced me to this incredible outdoor dining experience, one that I believe she arrived at as we do many recipes – out of necessity.

One afternoon in deer camp in her native Washington State, my wife found herself with a freshly harvested ruffed grouse and a hot bed of coals. Innovator that she is, she quickly cleaned the bird whole and rinsed it thoroughly with water from a nearby alpine stream. A little salt and pepper inside and out went on before a handful of apple and onion slices went in. The bird was then wrapped in a *triple* layer of heavy-duty aluminum foil.

A small depression was dug in the coals at the edge of the fire, and the tightly wrapped package placed in it. She then covered the bird with a six to eight-inch blanket of coals and left camp for the evening's blacktail hunt. At dark she returned, pulled the package from the coals, and unwrapped what she could describe only as the culinary equivalent of the best Christmas present she'd ever received.

"I'd never tasted anything like this bird," she told me years after the fact. "It was moist and juicy. Just falling off the bone. I don't think I'd ever had better, before or since." Cooking time? For this bird, about two hours; however, Julie warns soon-to-be campfire cooks that their cooking times may vary depending on their particular fire and subsequent bed of coals.

"It can take as little as an hour," she says. "Or as long as three or four. There's quite a bit of experimentation involved here. My theories are these – You can always add more time; you can't take away time once the bird's overdone. Too, if you're worried about the bird drying out, which is something you *don't* want to do, place three or four slices of fat bacon over the breast before you wrap it. And do wrap it well. Even a small 'leak' in the foil can cause moisture to be lost and the bird to eventually burn," she added.

Pheasant under (a) glass (lid)

First, roll the cleaned and dried pieces – breasts, thighs, or both – in seasoned flour. Put the coated pieces on a plate and place them in the 'fridge for 20 minutes or so. This allows the coating to set or stick to the pieces better during the browning process.

The next step is to brown each of the pieces, both sides. Once browned, transfer the pieces to a paper towel-covered plate and allow them to drain well. While the bird is draining, find that old crock-pot that you use but once a year. Which, by the way, is a real shame as crock-pots are actually quite wonderful things. And that glass cover? Yes, that's where the recipe gets its name. Original, eh? Oh, and before I forget. If you don't want to heat up the kitchen, or you're not into the semi-fried food thing, there's always the popular George Foreman Grill. Simply slap the seasoned pieces on ole' George, punch in three to four minutes, and close the lid. The result is Step One in the process, minus the oil, *and plus* those neat-looking grill marks that only George can apply. I'm getting teary-eyed now…

Anyway, let's assume you've found the crock-pot. Set it aside for a moment. Now in a mixing bowl, combine a can of Cream of Mushroom soup, three cups of orange juice, and a couple shakes of Watkins' garlic oil. If, like me, you like your recipes a bit on the spicy side, now's the time to add a dash or two of House of Tsang Hot Chili or Hot Sesame Oil. Or Tabasco. Or a diced cayenne or two. Anything that raises the mix to the temperature of your choosing. Now, too, is the time to add just a pinch of salt and a little fresh ground pepper. Maybe even a glug of red wine and a squirt of Worchestershire sauce. You see where I'm going here? Nowhere….that's why it's so simple. Once you've added the soup, the orange juice, and the garlic, the rest is up to you.

Once you've finished creating the liquid, now's the time to grab that bag of frozen stir-fry vegetables from the freezer. You know, it's the bag with the broccoli, cauliflower, water chestnuts, mushrooms, and a handful of other unidentified bits and pieces of good garden stuff. Pour a half-inch or so of the liquid into the crock pot and add a layer of pheasant. Next, add a layer of vegetables. Then add more liquid and another layer of pheasant. And so on and so on and so on until everything's gone. All that's left is to set the pot on low, and leave 'er sit for, oh, four hours. Maybe six. Honestly? Six hours is about the longest I've been able to stand smelling and *not* eating. You see how long you last.

9

Where have all the rabbit hunters gone?

Courtesy of Phil Bourjaily

The Hollanders - Father Will, and sons, Luke (center), and Hans. Doing their part in Iowa.

There was a time during the late 1960s and early 1970s as I was growing up in the northeastern corner of Ohio when the opening day of rabbit and pheasant season – November 15 – was every bit as popular as the opening day of deer season. Diners were full from the Ohio River to the Indiana state line, and the dress for the day was tattered brush pants, a pair of patched Northerner boots, a crusty and rather decrepit shell vest with one pocket missing, and a blaze orange hat – reversible to camouflage, of course. Every mid-70s model Ford F-100 came complete with a dog box, a Ziploc bag full of dog biscuits, a thermos of coffee, and a couple Moon Pies. This, after all, was rabbit season, a day as big or bigger than Christmas.

Today, unfortunately, November 15 is, well, November

15. For many hunters across the United States, it's simply the day that falls between the 14th and the 16th. In many parts of the country, the rabbit hunters are gone. They've simply vanished; much the same as does a fall flight of snipe following November's first good, hard freeze.

And why? For the most part, it's certainly not because there aren't any rabbits. In most parts of the country, and despite the increased human population and resulting encroachment upon wildlife habitat in general, eastern cottontail rabbit populations are as good or better than they were a decade ago. Sure, coyotes are enjoying a rabbit dinner on occasion. And without question, every state has a handful of red-tailed hawks that are very adept at filling their talons with fine-eating cottontail. But the fact remains that it's the rabbit hunters, not the rabbits, which have disappeared. Why?

Born and raised near Iowa City, Iowa, and some of the finest upland game hunting available in the United States, Dave Fountain, 38, has several theories of his own as to why rabbit hunters have gone the way of the great auk and the Labrador teal. Brought up in a hunting household by an avid pheasant hunter and houndsman, Fountain cut his teeth on rabbits and, as many hunters across the nation did, fox squirrels. Now living just a short drive north of his hometown, Fountain, a beagle man like his father, is raising his son, Tyler, 16, in a manner that he refers to as traditional, and in very much the same way as his father did him. And herein lies the first of his reasons behind the decline of the rabbit hunter.

"When you and I were younger, we'd go to school on Monday and talk to all our friends about how our hunting went over the weekend. This was from about sixth grade on. That just doesn't happen anymore. I just don't think that the fathers are introducing their children to hunting at a young age. My son at 16 is one of only two kids in his entire tenth grade class who does hunt with his father. It's just not something that happens," said Fountain.

And he continues by saying that while there are young people who do hunt, it's not for rabbits or squirrels, but something much more popular by today's hunting standards.

"The kids nowadays, and when I say kids I'm talking about those young people 18 years old and younger, that do hunt, hunt what I consider to be the 'glory' game. They hunt the rooster pheasants because they can go out in a group and hunt with a dog, and there's something in people's eyes these days that's perhaps more prestigious about shooting a rooster pheasant than a rabbit. Look at the number of people who hunt deer and nothing but deer. They own one gun and it's an 870 Special Purpose slug gun, and that's all they hunt. And I'm talking about people our age who have never even hunted a rabbit (because) they're deer hunters," he continued.

Two states to the east of The Hawkeye State, Chip

Claudia's taking her role as driver seriously. Dan Donarski and Gary Howey, too, look upon their role as teacher with great importance.

Gross, now retired special projects coordinator for the Ohio Department of Natural Resources (ODNR), Division of Wildlife, echoes Fountain's sentiments concerning the change in hunter trends.

"People have made the transition from small game to big game or, if they're young hunters, they've already had the opportunity to hunt big game such as whitetails. And that makes something like hunting rabbits seem a lot less glamorous," said Gross.

It makes sense. In states like Ohio where the current whitetail population pushes the half million mark, there was a time when seeing a deer track or, Heaven forbid, an actual deer was cause enough to contact the local newspaper. But in the early 1980s, things changed in The Buckeye State, and seeing whitetails, as well as other novelty species like Canada geese and wild turkeys, became common, everyday events. So, too, did the opportunities to hunt these wonderful new game animals. Unfortunately, the increase in the popularity of these species led to a corresponding, although somewhat expected, decrease in the number of hunters pursuing small game species such as squirrels and, yes, cottontail rabbits.

"It's unfortunate that more people, especially young hunters, don't hunt rabbits. In small game hunting, these young hunters will have many opportunities to be placed or place themselves in "shoot/don't shoot" situations, whereas in big game hunting scenarios, hunters are often limited to one or two shots per season. From an outdoor

Courtesy of Warren H. Gross

The late Richard Gross, with his grandson, Andy. This, folks, is what it's all about.

A bright young man, Nick Miller's on his way to becoming a fine hunter and outdoorsman, thanks in large part to the teaching and support of his folks, Tony and Kerri.

education standpoint, small game hunting like rabbit or squirrel hunting is a wonderful teaching tool," said Gross.

But, says Gross, there may be other factors, which have contributed to the decline in the number of rabbit hunters in the United States.

"Habitat, or more precisely, a change in habitat has also had an impact on the number of rabbit hunters across the country. For that matter, all upland game hunters. We're seeing upland habitats decreasing, while at the same time forested habitats are on the rise in terms of area. And because of this change, hunters are having an easier time finding places to hunt forest-based game such as white-tails or wild turkeys, and a correspondingly more difficult time locating those upland habitats which still sustain a population of species such as cottontails, pheasants, and quail," said Gross.

Still, and despite the downward spiral into which it would seem the country's rabbit hunting population has fallen, there are still those who want nothing more than to see a thin skim of frost on a field of goldenrod and hear the bawl of a beagle dog hot on the trail of a bunny. Just recently, my wife and I, along with my father and a former student of his, spent a pair of very eventful days in the southeastern corner of Iowa hunting pheasants. There, at the "hot water or heat, but not both" motel that we've stayed in for the past two years, we had the pleasure of meeting and talking with not one or two, but 18 wonderful Southern gentlemen who, along with their 20 beagles, had

made the 16-hour drive from their home in eastern North Carolina specifically to hunt Hawkeye State bunnies.

And hunt bunnies, they did. When we arrived on Wednesday, the group had just finished the day's hunt. Total bag – 30 cottontails. Thursday's take wasn't as good, I was told, when we had returned from our foray into the uplands. "We only got 14 today," said one of the young men.

"Oh, we've been coming here for about six or seven years now," said the one gentleman when I asked. We were packed, the black labs were in the kennel, and the truck was pointed north for the return trip home. "And we'll be back next year. Same time, same place. There just ain't nothing like this rabbit hunting to relax a man. It does his soul good."

And it must because every last briar-scratched, hot, and dusty one of them was smiling.

Through their eyes –

Just what is the future of small game hunting? Or for that matter, does it have a future? Wanting to close this book on a positive note, I want to say – "Why, yes. Certainly it does." Still, there's a part of me, maybe that infernal realistic part of me, that keeps whispering in my ear things like – "When was the last time you saw a squirrel hunter in the woods, M.D.?" Or – "You hear about rabbit hunters. But who was the last rabbit hunter you talked with in the field? Huh?"

I hate to say this, but I'm not sure there's a definitive answer to this one. In parts of the country, as I've already mentioned, squirrel and rabbit hunting are still popular. Men and boys travel great distances, beagles in tow, simply for the thrill of the chase, and Grandpas and grandsons sit, side-by-side, under towering oaks and century-old maples, all on the off-chance that they'll see a fox squirrel. What they know without question, these lost-artisans, is that they'll share something special.

But as I'm not one to settle for – "I don't know" – I asked a handful of folks for their answer to my question: What is the future of small game hunting? Hopefully, you'll find their responses of interest; but more importantly, I hope you'll take them to heart.

Brad Harris, VP of public relations for Outland Sports

We're hung up on big game. We're hung on whitetails and turkeys. And I've made that mistake…Or rather, I made that choice with my oldest son that when he started hunting, I took him out on the deer and the turkey because they were the high-profile animals. That's what people wanted to read about. That was the big excitement.

But when you do that, you miss out on a lot of learning skills and the passion that small game hunting brings to the hunt. To me, when you hunt small game like squirrels and rabbits, you're hunting for the sport of hunting. They're not perceived as the glamour species – the wide antlers or the long spurs. So when you're hunting things like squirrels and rabbits, you're not hunting them for the antlers or the beard length, but you're hunting them out of the passion for the hunt. Just to be afield.

I think that by starting at a young age and with small game, you get that true passion for the outdoors. And you never forget it. I know the guys I know who started out hunting small game and now are avid big game hunters still hunt squirrels. And it's not that way with people who start hunting deer and turkeys 'cause I think that they think it's a step backwards. In reality, it's not. It's a step forward.

Right now, we **do** need to make a conscious effort as sportsmen to instill the tradition of small game hunting simply because everything else will build on that. By starting with small game, we can keep the hunting tradition alive. Big game and everything else – it'll just fall into place. So we need to make that conscious effort, with the kids and with the ladies. We need to show them that hunting is a passion **not** a trophy. It's (small game hunting) is the greatest teaching tool that we have available to us

Phil Bourjaily, shotgunning editor for Field & Stream

If you're talking about small game hunting you're

Gordon Bourjaily, 14, and his buddy, Ike. Our hunting future rests in the hands of talented young men like Gordon. Does he have your support?

going to have to divide it up. The future of upland bird hunting is pretty strong because there's a tradition in the industry behind it. The one that we're losing is the squirrel hunting and the rabbit hunting which is, for whatever reason, not as glamorous. That's what's dying out. I think we'll always have bird hunting, but the squirrel and the rabbit hunting… those are the things that I think are in danger of fading away. And I think they're important – and you and I have talked about this – I think it's important for kids to go because… I mean, shooting anything for a kid is exciting, but if you don't shoot a rabbit or a squirrel, there'll be another one along. That's just not the case with deer and turkeys, and I think it's (small game hunting) a great low-pressure way to start hunting. It's a great way too, I think, for kids to start hunting on their own when they're old enough and responsible enough to do that. I might not want to send a kid off on his own to deer hunt or to turkey hunt, but rabbits and squirrels. You grew up that way, and when I started hunting it was later in life but I started the same way by going out and chasing rabbits and squirrels around.

You can argue that there's no reason not to start your kids on deer and turkeys except that it introduces pressure at an early age. And I think that's wrong. I mean, we start kids too soon on serious athletics. We start kids too soon on everything these days, and I think there should be more time to be a kid. And if that means just screwing around in the woods and squirrel hunting, then that's important.

Courtesy of Toxey Haas and Mossy Oak

Mossy Oak founder, Toxey Haas, believes strongly in his role as mentor and educator…and passer of the torch to the next generation.

Chip Gross, retired wildlife and education officer with the Ohio Division of Wildlife

So many people today have switched to big game hunting, but there's a ton of small game out there. And it is, as we've talked before, a great way to start young people out hunting.

I don't know how we shift people back that way or get them thinking back that way. Hopefully this book will do some of that. There's just some tremendous opportunities here, and often, it's very close to home. You don't have to travel like you often do when you hunt big game.

I don't know how many people actually sit down and consciously think about passing along this tradition. When my Dad taught me to hunt, I don't think it was a conscious decision like 'Okay, I'm going to teach my son to hunt small game now.' He was a hunter himself and he just took me along, which was what Dads and kids did at that age and time. I picked it up that way. And I'm sure that a lot of kids decided that they didn't like it and

went on to other things.

But I think it is more of a conscious effort now-a-days than it was in the last generation. And I think it has to be because there are so many things competing for kids' time that as hunters, if we want to see that tradition continued, then we're going to have to make more of a concerted effort to do that. And the reason that's important is not just so we can say we have hunters today like we did generations ago. Hunters and anglers, when you look at the statistics today, are more concerned about natural resources than any other part of the population. Why? Because they put their money where their mouth is. That money goes to licenses, which in turn goes back into conservation agencies who in their turn manage the wildlife. That, I think, is one of the main reasons why we have to be concerned because in the long run, the resources will suffer if the consumptive user of wildlife disappears.

Buck Gardner, World Duck Calling Champion (1994), and Champion of Champions (1995)

Squirrel hunting is where I started. Rabbit hunting. Dove hunting. A little bit of quail hunting. But it was something that we could go out and do 'cause there was a lot of available space. I think part of the problem today is that there's just not that same kind of space and that same kind of opportunity for youngsters to get out and do it. So folks like me, we have to get them out there and get them involved in it.

And…you know, M.D., I'm just saying this from my heart. We all lead such busy lives, and we have such passions for the pursuits that we do have – you know for me, it's waterfowling – that we don't take a lot of time for the other stuff. But like today, there's this friend of mine and I took his son bream fishing. And he's hooked. He can't wait to go back. And he's looking at finding out about a hunter education course because he wants to go duck hunting. But do we do enough of it? No, we don't. And the blame falls squarely on the shoulders of people like me and you. The success or the failure of it. You know, my Dad took the time to take me fishing and hunting. And he took my friends hunting and fishing. And he **made** time to do it. I'd like to think I do a lot of it, but I probably need to do a lot more –

Toxey Haas, founder of Mossy Oak brand camouflage –

Turkey hunting is my favorite sport. I don't consider turkeys big game 'cause big game in my mind is something where the trophy is more important than the meat. And that's what I have a problem with. I'm more into game management than I am hunting – almost. I love growing whatever. I love wildlife. If you want to characterize me, it's not some big game hunter. I don't ever want to be known as that. I'm a nature lover. I'm a nature freak. I just love the woods.

And so I'll get right to the point of what you'll get out of me and small game hunting. The value of that squirrel is just the same as that 180-class deer. And I think we've lost that. And the social specialness of hunting seems to get lost 'cause it's become so individualized to 'Hey, I shot this big deer.' You know, these squirrel hunts and rabbit hunts and dove hunts are a part of our culture here in the South. And it's very valuable, but it's slipping all the time.

We're moving our hunting culture to where it's all about the result and not the experience. With small game, it's more about the 'getting to go hunting' than it is about the results. Nobody wants to teach kids anymore. All you see written is what the deer scored. I hate the score card on hunting.

Rob Keck, CEO for the National Wild Turkey Federation (NWTF).

In today's hunting fraternity, we have probably done a disservice to our future hunters by really putting too much emphasis on the trophy aspect of what it is they're hunting instead of the trophy quality time that they need to be spending out there afield learning basic skills, learning basic concepts, responsibility, ectera. And I look at this in the face of tremendous opportunity and small game resources which are absolutely underutilized.

In today's kind of fast food society, I think that we have really tried to get instant gratification by putting a kid on a deer stand where he's going to kill a humungous buck the first time out. And he's gone to graduate school before he's gone to elementary school. I think that we really need to back up and look and see what or how these hunters of the Baby Boomer Generation got involved and how they really developed their love of hunting and their love of the out-of-doors. I think I'm probably an example, like many. I mean, I carried a dang pop-gun and was just barely able to walk, but man I cried at times when my Dad and my Granddad and my uncles wouldn't take me along with 'em. And how I had that burning desire to go out there.

I really think that today, we have not given young hunters what we need to give them for the future. Those building blocks that are going to carry them and make them experienced woodsmen. To be able to handle all kinds of challenges and situations. I think that we have to show them that we don't measure success the size of the trophy, but rather by the size of the experience. And a trophy experience is what we're looking for. I look so often at the times I go back to places where I hunted as a kid and I think about those times when I just wanted

The NWTF is one of our country's biggest proponents of youth and their role in the outdoors, and Rob Keck (black vest, left), one of the movement's foremost leaders.

to spend that quality time with someone else instead of making them sit endless hours on a deer stand, and making them pass up buck after buck after buck because he's not as wide as his ears or he doesn't have eight points. I think we're absolutely killing the excitement and the thrill of the hunt by putting our emphasis in the wrong places.

If you look toward the future, it's going to be really, really important that we emphasize the importance of starting out with basic small game hunting. Period.

Orlan Love, outdoor writer for The Gazette (Cedar Rapids, Iowa)

I think small game does have a future, and the reason I think that, M.D., is because of the increasing competition for places to hunt the more glamorous game animals like turkey and deer and pheasants. There's very little hunting pressure on rabbits and squirrels, and I think people that are maybe getting squeezed out of these other sports are going to take up small game hunting.

I was talking just a week or so ago to a friend of mine who lives in Jesup (Iowa). He has a son who's in high school. He was telling me that in the last few years, they've really concentrated their hunting for squirrels and rabbits during January and February. And he told me that the reason they did that was because there's very little competi-

It's been shown that families who hunt together interact more positively with one another on a daily basis.

tion for places to hunt and for the game itself. He tells me that they have no problem getting permission from landowners to go in and hunt rabbits and squirrels. They're finding abundant populations of both, and they like to eat rabbits and squirrels. It's a good sport for them. Just a good chance to spend time together.

I think that young kids are getting recruited into hunting, but it's not coming in small game. It's coming in deer and turkeys. All the young guys that we hunt with have really cut their spurs hunting turkeys and deer. I guess I don't see a big problem with that as long as they're learning the fundamentals of the sport. How to do it safely, and to appreciate the game that they're after. I guess it doesn't make that much difference to me whether they do it with deer and turkey or squirrel and rabbit.

Rob Paradise, sales manager for Flambeau Products

When I think of small game for what I do (decoy design, manufacture, and promotion), that means squirrel, rabbit, and dove. Mostly dove. The nice thing here is that all three species are easy for a kid to get into. It's like the ultimate starting point for a child. You don't need a heavy barrel. You don't need the bigger gauges. It's just easy and simple for them to get into.

Enjoyment. That's probably the most important part of small game hunting – is to make it enjoyable. If you make it enjoyable, then the kids are going to stay involved and – hopefully – go on to other forms of hunting.

I think one of the main things is the fact that you just don't hear about dove or rabbit hunting anymore. And I'm guilty of this, but when I think of rabbit hunters, I think of old-timers. Why? Because they're not in the limelight. All you hear about is turkey and deer, and maybe to some extent, waterfowl, but every magazine you look at is telling you 'Ten Ways to Stalk a Deer' or 'Five Mistakes Made in a Treestand.' Everything is getting a huge buck or a big turkey. There's glory and glamour in that, and I just think that when that's all you see in the magazines, there's no hype about squirrel hunting or rabbit hunting to get the kids into it. And that's the fault of the father or whoever's taking them hunting.

Ernie Calandrelli, Quaker Boy Game Calls public relations manager

My eyes were opened after I had kids. Of course, I grew up small game hunting with my Dad, and that's how I was introduced to the outdoors. That tuned me in to what was out there. Of course, we didn't have video games back then, but I would just as soon – back then – go out into the woods and *watch* my father hunt squirrels and learn about the outdoors.

And I believe we're losing a lot of kids nowadays to

the video games and sitting around watching TV. Another thing that jumps into my mind is baseball. During the summer, I used to play baseball from daylight 'til dark. Now, my kid plays on two baseball teams, and the only time he plays is when either the coach calls a practice or they have a game night. Other than that, he's looking for something to do. Luckily, he's not one of those kids to sit there and play computer games or what-have-you.

You know, we are in a shrinking industry right now, and it's just going to keep on shrinking. And besides the kids not getting into the outdoors, they're not going to know anything about the outdoors. They're not going to realize what they have out there to enjoy, whether this is in the world of hunting and fishing, or just getting out there to take a nature walk. To know an oak tree from a maple tree. Or to know this bush from that type of bush.

Right after my son was born, right away what jumped into my mind were the years that I spent with my Dad squirrel hunting. And that's exactly what I do with him now. By taking him into the woods and teaching him how to squirrel hunt – or actually, by letting him make a lot of the mistakes on his own, he learned the skills that were available to him. And this just progressed into the other things that he enjoys hunting.

I know my boy's lucky in a lot of ways 'cause he gets to go a lot of places with me, but to give you some idea of what's happening here. Normally, he hunts deer with me in the Midwest every year. He just turned 11, and this fall, I gave him an option. I asked him, 'What do you want to do this Fall?' You know what he told me? He told me that he wanted to go on a duck hunt.

Let me tell you. I just love going into the woods with my kids. You talk about bonding experiences? There is no better bonding experience.

Jim Wentz, Hunter Education Consultant

When I grew up in the late 1950s and early 60s, people hunted a lot of different small game. And then as deer came on, they did some deer hunting too. Today, most people are specialists. They specialize in deer or they specialize in turkey. And that has some management implications that people should be concerned about. One is the generalists usually were open to types of regulations that benefit ecosystems overall versus some of the specialist organizations that put pressure on to manage for one certain species.

I think another thing that makes it harder for people to hunt small game today is that a lot of it requires the use of dogs or additional equipment. And a lot of people live in smaller places, especially people of hunting age. They move around a lot because of jobs and training, and they're living in apartments or condos. They live in places

No car? Not a problem for up-and-coming trapper, Tyler Fountain. This IS our future. It's your obligation to stand behind him.

where it's hard to keep hunting dogs and it's hard to keep a wide variety of hunting equipment and clothing and decoys and all those different things we need.

The biggest thing for the future of all hunting is that kids need to be surrounded by social support for hunting in order for them to develop their awareness and interest in it. Social support is seeing all your friends and your family, teachers, and people in your community hunting. And in different parts of the country, that social support is disappearing. The support for hunting isn't gone, but kids just don't grow up seeing the hunting activity around them in the way that they used to. I think that in those parts of the country where there still is a lot of hunting activity and it's fairly rural, kids are being exposed to that social support. In fact, studies say that kids exposed to this support are just as interested today as they used to be.

Society has changed a lot in the last several decades in how they look at recreation time, as well as in the number of recreational opportunities available – especially for kids. Primarily now, kids do a lot of different things. They do them in short lots of time, and parents are more 'schedulers.' They take one child and drop them off at soccer. Another child they drop off at dance class. Then they go back to the first one and take them to a different activity. There's a lot more that, where parents and immediate family members aren't so much introducing the kids to the recreational time as they are scheduling it. Time plays into this, too. With kids, they tend to jump into something, do

What is Claudia learning here as she follows her Dad, Dr. A.J. Cummings, during a pheasant hunt in South Dakota? The truth is any of 1,001 different things, and it would be a shame if she missed even one.

Trapping has become a lost art, particularly among our country's youth. But there is time for change; however, that time is now.

What does the future hold for our next generation of hunters? Shouldn't we be helping define that future....now?

it for two hours, and they're ready to move onto the next thing. That's just the way we've acclimated them. And hunting is different. It takes time to get ready. It takes time to travel to the hunting location. It requires time in the woods. So that's just another element to deal with.

I think that for people who want to introduce their own children (to hunting), or to work with other kids, the future may lie in clubs like the 4-H Shooting Sports Club. Ideally, you can bring together kids and their family members in groups, and maybe you have a specialist who can share places and expertise and knowledge to help present a well rounded outdoor experience.

Karen Roop, editor of Women in the Outdoors Magazine –

A lot of the articles that are being presented to me and we're running in *Women in the Outdoors* magazine are using the small game species to introduce people to hunting. And mostly it's squirrels and squirrel hunting 'cause you don't have to be all clad in camo in order to go and it's

something where you're using a non-intimidating firearm to do it. And you can just kind of walk around. Overall, it's not intimidating like if you're showering down with a scent killer to go on a deer hunt or the intensity of a bow hunt. It's (small game) something where you can socialize and – well – have fun. That's not to say that big game hunting isn't fun, only that small game hunting might be less intimidating.

Reading other women's experiences, whether that be dove hunting or quail hunting or pheasant hunting, leads me to the camaraderie that goes along with small game hunting. Walking around in the field with a group of people as you hunt. I think that in and of itself is key for women because that's why a lot of women want to get involved in hunting activities. It's not necessarily out of the trophy aspect of hunting or proving themselves to their friends and families, but rather just spending time with them. It's the social aspect of hunting, and I think that's key with a lot of your small game species.

Appendix I

Agencies, outfitters, and manufacturers

I've said this before, but, the way I see it, if it's worth saying once, it's definitely worth saying again. Just ask the folks who have tired of me saying things twice; however, I digress. What I've said before is this – One of the nicest things about small game hunting is the simplicity. Still, this isn't to say that there aren't at least a handful of things,

call it *stuff* if you will or *gear* if you must, that can or do make any small game hunting venture either a little more productive, a bit more pleasant, or a little of both.

That said, I'd like to, as Jim Schoby was so very fond of saying, give a tip of the 'ole hunting cap to the folks who make *The Stuff*.

Arborwear
PO Box 341
Chagrin Falls, OH 44022
1-888-578-TREE
www.arborwear.com

Flambeau Products
PO Box 97
Middlefield, OH 44062
www.flamprod.com

**Remington Arms
Company**
870 Remington Dr.
Madison, NC 27025
www.remington.com

Winchester
427 N. Shamrock St.
East Alton, IL 49685
www.winchester.com

Browning
One Browning Place
Morgan, UT 84050
www.browning.com

MAD Calls, A division of
Outland Sports
4500 Doniphan Dr.
Neosho, MO 64850
www.outland-sports.com

Lohman Game Calls, A
division of Outland
Sports
4500 Doniphan Dr.
Neosho, MO 64850
www.outland-sports.com

Mossy Oak Clothing –
Haas Outdoors
PO Box 757
West Point, MS 39773
www.mossyoak.com

**Realtree Outdoor
Products, Inc.**
PO Box 9638
Columbus, GA 31908
www.realtree.com

**Federal Cartridge
Company** (Blount, Inc.)
900 Ehlen Dr.
Anoka, MN 55303
www.federalcartridge.com

DeLorme Mapping
Two Delorme Dr.
Yarmouth, ME 04096
www.delorme.com

**Rocky Shoes & Boots,
Inc.**
39 Canal St.
Nelsonville, OH 45764
www.rockyboots.com

C.C. Filson
PO Box 34020
Seattle, WA 98124
www.filson.com

**Columbia Sportswear
Company**
6600 N. Baltimore
Portland, OR 97283
www.columbia.com

Bushnell Sports Optics
9200 Cody
Overland Park, KS 66214
www.bushnell.com

Nikon Sport Optics
1300 Walt Whitman Rd.
Melville, NY 11747
www.nikonusa.com

Bass Pro Shops
2500 E. Kearney
Springfield, MO 65898
www.basspro.com

Cabela's
One Cabela's Drive
Sidney, NE 69160
www.cabelas.com

Birchwood Casey
7900 Fuller Rd.
Eden Prairie, MN 55344
www.birchwoodcasy.com

Burnham Brothers
PO Box 1148
Menard, TX 76859
www.burnhambrothers.com

Bug-Out Outdoorwear
22111 230th Ave.
Centerville, IA 52544
*www.bug-out-outdoor-
wear.com*

Ralston Purina
Checkerboard Square
St. Louis, MO 63164
1-800-7-PURINA

Avery Outdoors
PO Box 820176
Memphis, TN 38112
901-324-1500
www.averyoutdoors.com

Quaker Boy Game Calls
5455 Webster Rd.
Orchard Park, NY 14127
*www.quakerboygame-
calls.com*

**Gerber Legendary
Blades**
14200 SW 72nd Ave.
Portland, OR 97223
www.gerberblades.com

**Knight & Hale Game
Calls**
Drawer 670
Cadiz, KY 42211
www.knight-hale.com

Tender Corporation
PO Box 290
Littleton Industrial Park
Littleton, NH 03561
www.tendercorp.com

Hunter's Specialties
6000 Huntington Ct. NE
Cedar Rapids, IA 52402
www.hunterspec.com

**Kent Cartridge America,
Inc.**
PO Box 849
Kearneysville, WV 25430
www.kentgamebore.com

Regional, state, and local agencies

One of the things that I like best about small game hunting is that in most cases the opportunity exists right next door. However, there are those times when the quest for a particular adventure or species takes one across state lines. And while hunting on the road is certainly enjoyable, it's not without its long-distance logistical considerations.

Enter – these folks. These folks, as I call them, are the men and women of the various state fish and wildlife agencies, travel and tourism departments, and convention bureaus, who dedicate their 40-hour week to seeing that tens of thousands of personal sojourns go off without a

hitch. You need a map? They have maps. Looking for a bed? They'll have a list of every enclosed area ranging from the local No-tell Motel to the very best in five-star accommodations. Wanna know where the birds are? Chances are good that there's someone in the office who hunts and is willing to spend some phone time with you. They're an untapped and – unfortunately – often unrecognized valuable resource for the hunter on the move. And with that in mind, Julie and I would like to personally thank the following folks for helping this book make the metamorphosis from dream to reality. Again, Jim Schoby's "Tip of the 'Ole Hunting Cap" to –

Nebraska Division of Travel & Tourism
PO Box 98907
Lincoln, NE 68509
877-NEBRASKA
www.visitnebraska.org

Minnesota Office of Tourism
100 Metro Square,
121 7th Place East
St. Paul, MN 55101
800-657-3638
www.travelks.org

South Dakota Department of Tourism
711 E. Wells Ave.
Pierre, SD 57501
800-S-DAKOTA
www.travelsd.com

Kansas Department of Wildlife and Parks
512 SE 25th Ave.
Pratt, KS 67124
620-672-5911
www.kdwp.state.ks.us

Kansas Travel & Tourism
Kansas Department of Commerce & Housing
800-2-KANSAS
www.travelks.org

Trumbull County Convention & Visitor's Bureau
650 Youngstown-Warren Rd.
Niles, OH 44446
800-672-9555
www.trumbullcountycvb.org

North Dakota Game & Fish Department
100 N. Bismarck Expressway
Bismarck, ND 58501

Klickitat County Tourism
127 W. Court St.
Goldendale, WA 98620
509-773-7060
www.klickitatcountry.org /tourism

Springfield Convention & Visitors Bureau
3315 E. Battlefield Rd.
Springfield, MO 65804
800-678-8767
www.springfieldmo.org

Long Beach Visitor's Bureau
PO Box 562
Long Beach, WA 98631
www.funbeach.com

Outfitters

It's only been within the past five years that I've really come to know some of the folks who call themselves outfitters. And along the way, I've had both the pleasure and the honor of meeting some very outstanding people. And, via that same path, I've come into contact with, how shall I say, some very interesting individuals – folks who perhaps should be doing something other than guiding hunters…anything, as long as it has nothing to do with people and the possession of people skills. Know what I mean?

But a good outfitter – a Delten Rhoades or a Richard Kieffer, for instance – can be as integral a part of the hunting experience as a keen-nosed hound or a finely-balanced shotgun. You see these folks are more than just finders of game. They're leaders. And they're educators. They're safety instructors, storytellers, and entertainers.

To many, they're role models. With few exceptions, those I've met are to be admired and envied in the same instant. But they can't change the weather. And they can't make the pheasants fly any more slowly. And – sorry to say – they can't do a thing about the fact that you haven't picked up a shotgun in the past 11 months.

Below is just a partial list of the hundreds of noteworthy small game and upland bird guides currently operating in the United States. Much better and more complete listings can be found in such publications as the North American Hunting Club's Resource Directory (www.huntingclub.com), or *Black's Wing & Clay Shotgunner's Handbook* (732-224-8700). I've personally hunted with the following folks, and they're not only professionals in a business sense, but they're just flat fun to be around.

Sandhills Adventures
Delten & Tracy Rhoades
PO Box 152
Brewster, NE 68821
www.sandhills-adventures.com
Pheasants, sharptails, prairie chickens, ducks, geese, coyotes, deer, turkeys

Bill Bruns
Bruns Farms Hunts
10607 397th Ave.
Hecla, SD 57446
605-885-6324
www.angelfire.com/sd2/brunsfarms
Pheasants, ducks, geese, swans, deer, buffalo

Richard & Diana Kieffer
Kieffer Pheasant Hunting
37361 257th St.
White Lake, SD 57383
605-249-2464
www.kiefferhunting.com
Pheasants

Rock Creek Lodge
Dennis & Rod Brakke
24935 416th Ave.
Fulton, SD 57340
605-996-9301
www.southdakotapheasants.com

Funkrest, Inc.
Don & Bonnie Funk
RR 3, Box 167
Madison, SD 57042
605-256-3636

Mallardith NW Adventures
Bruce Meredith
81025 E. Wpainitia Rd.
Maupin, OR 97037
541-980-1922
www.mallardith.com
Pheasants, quail, chukars, Huns, ducks, geese

Arrowhead Hunt Club
Dan Mullin
3529 170th St.
Goose Lake, IA 52750
563-577-2267
Pheasant, quail, chukar

Running Spring Farm
Bill Cork
PO Box 105
Everton, MO 65646
417-535-4190
www.runningspringfarm.com
Pheasants, chukar

Conservation and related organizations

It's all about volunteers donating their time, money, and sweat equity in order to provide opportunities for wildlife, hunters, and non-consumptive outdoor enthusiasts all across the country. You're benefiting. Are these organizations benefiting from your contributions?

Ruffed Grouse Society
451 McCormick Rd.
Corapolis, PA 15108
www.ruffedgrousesociety.com

Quail Unlimited
PO Box 610
Edgefield, SC 29824
803-637-5731
www.qu.org

Pheasants Forever
1783 Buerkle Circle
St. Paul, MN 55110
www.pheasantsforever.org

National Wild Turkey Federation
770 Augusta Rd.
Edgefield, SC 29824
www.nwtf.org

Beagles Unlimited
12703 Via Posada Way
Victorville, CA 92392
www.beaglesunlimited.com

Dove Sportsmen's Society
31 Quail Run
Edgefield, SC 29824
803-637-5731
www.qu.org

National Trappers Association
PO Box 632018
Nacogdoches, TX 75963
www.nationaltrappers.com
E-mail:
TRAPPERS@aol.com